WEAPON

NAMBU PISTOLS

JOHN WALTER

Series Editor Martin Pegler

Illustrated by Adam Hook & Alan Gilliland

OSPREY PUBLISHING
Bloomsbury Publishing Plc
Kemp House, Chawley Park, Cumnor Hill, Oxford OX2 9PH, UK
29 Earlsfort Terrace, Dublin 2, Ireland
1385 Broadway, 5th Floor, New York, NY 10018, USA
E-mail: info@ospreypublishing.com
www.ospreypublishing.com

OSPREY is a trademark of Osprey Publishing Ltd

First published in Great Britain in 2023

A catalog record for this book is available from the
British Library.

ISBN: PB 9781472855428; eBook 9781472855435;
ePDF 9781472855442; XML 9781472855411

23 24 25 26 27   10 9 8 7 6 5 4 3 2 1

Index by Rob Munro
Typeset by PDQ Digital Media Solutions, Bungay, UK
Printed and bound in India by Replika Press Private Ltd.

Osprey Publishing supports the Woodland Trust, the UK's
leading woodland conservation charity.

To find out more about our authors and books visit
www.ospreypublishing.com. Here you will find extracts, author
interviews, details of forthcoming events and the option to sign
up for our newsletter.

Front cover, above: "Grandpa" Nambu 719, with its holster
stock attached to the butt-heel lug. (Rock Island Auction,
www.rockislandauction.com)

Front cover, below: Special Naval Landing Forces personnel with
a variety of weapons. One of the men emerging under the sidecar
wields a 14th Year Type pistol while his companion appears to have
a Luger. (The Tank Museum, Bovington, www.tankmuseum.org)

Title-page photo: A Japanese soldier in cold-weather gear holds
a 14th Year Type pistol of the pre-1940 "small guard" type, the
holster being visible beside his right elbow. The size of his gloved
finger shows why the 14th Year Type trigger guard had to be
enlarged for use in cold temperatures. (Author's archives)

Dedication

To Alison, Adam, Nicky, Findlay, Georgia, Holly and the
menagerie!

Acknowledgments

Any attempt to chronicle the Nambu pistols' history inevitably
has to acknowledge work undertaken, in particular, by Frederick
Leithe and Harry Derby and more recently by James Brown,
whose *Collector's Guide to Imperial Japanese Handguns 1893–
1945* has proved indispensable: I am pleased to add my
appreciation of their pioneering contributions.

I have also been privileged to refer to the work of Robert
Kenneth Wilson, author of *Textbook of Automatic Pistols*. This
groundbreaking study was originally published in 1943, but
reprinted in 1975 at a time when I was working for its publisher.
When Wilson, a highly qualified surgeon whose career included
combat with British Army Special Forces during World War II,
retired as Chief Medical Officer of New Guinea he was able to
devote his time to preparing a sequel to *Textbook of Automatic
Pistols* entitled *Low Velocity Automatic Arms*. This never
appeared in print, but some copies seem to have been circulated
among Wilson's friends.

Robert Wilson died in 1969, but much of his archive was
acquired by the renowned writer Ian Hogg. Ian and I enjoyed a
friendly relationship for many years, and among materials that
changed hands between us during the compilation of *Japanese
Infantry Weapons of World War Two* (1976) was Chapter Ten of
Low Velocity Automatic Arms, "The Japanese Group of Pistols."
This dealt in copious detail with the several Nambu patterns,
14th Year Type, and Type 94 pistols, and proved indispensable.
I am grateful to James Wilson and Peter Phillips, grandson and
grandson-in-law of "RKW," for permission to use material from
Low Velocity Automatic Arms.

In addition, I must acknowledge a debt to the painstaking
serial-number/date correlation prepared by Mike and Dan Larkin
which appears on Teri Bryant's incredibly detailed Nambu World
website (http://www.nambuworld.com) and the work of
individual enthusiasts that can be found on http://www.
banzaionline.com.

My thanks are also due to the individuals and agencies who
supplied many excellent images and filled gaps in my knowledge:
Sarah Stoltzfus and Les Jones of Morphy Auctions; Matt Parise
of Rock Island Auctions; Rory Holloway and Greta Wass of the
Australian War Memorial; Bernhard Pacher of Hermann
Historica; Jenny Olech of Amoskeag Auctions; Steve Lansdale of
Heritage Auctions; Scott Benedict of Pre-98 Antiques; Vern
Easley; C. Peter Chen of World War II Database (https://ww2db.
com); peashooter85 and saigon1965 at https://www.tumblr.com;
and The Tank Museum at Bovington, Dorset, UK.

Artist's note

Readers may care to note that the original paintings from which
the color plates in this book were prepared are available for
private sale. All reproduction copyright whatsoever is retained by
the publishers. All inquiries should be addressed to:

scorpiopaintings@btinternet.com

The publishers regret that they can enter into no correspondence
upon this matter.

CONTENTS

INTRODUCTION

Even though the origins of gunpowder are often said to lie in China and its use in rockets, handguns were unknown in Japan until Portuguese adventurers, seeking to forge trade links, came ashore on the island of Tanegashima in 1543. With them they brought the matchlock firearms that were to inspire Japanese to copy them for centuries.

Apart from a limited amount of trade undertaken with the Netherlands through an enclave in Japan, very little else happened until the visits of the US Navy's Commodore Matthew Calbraith Perry and his squadron in the 1850s. Perry had been charged by US President Millard Fillmore with ensuring that Japanese ports were opened to trade, using force if necessary. Reaching Uraga in Edō Bay on July 8, 1853, Perry fired blanks from the 73 cannon of the steam frigate USS *Mississippi* to intimidate *shōgun* Tokugawa Ieyoshi. The letter Perry had been ordered to deliver was ultimately accepted by the *shōgun*'s representatives and Perry left, returning in February 1854 with ten ships, and was allowed to land at Kanagawa on March 8. A guard of honor provided by the local *daimyo* (master), carrying little other than matchlocks and polearms, contrasted so greatly with the US sailors and Marines and their cap-lock muskets to illustrate how far largely feudal Japan had fallen behind technologically. When efforts were made to overthrow the ruling Tokugawa shogunate and reinstate imperial rule, therefore, participants had to acquire weapons from European sources.

Primitive *tanegashima* matchlocks were undoubtedly used by the shogunate during the Boshin War (1868–69), but most troops used smoothbore muskets. Large numbers of these had reached Japan since the 17th century, and numerous types of more or less modern smoothbore muskets and rifles were imported from countries such as France, Germany, the Netherlands, Britain, and the United States. The first modern firearms in Japan seem to have been flintlocks imported about 1840 from the Netherlands by the samurai, military engineer, and pro-Western reformist

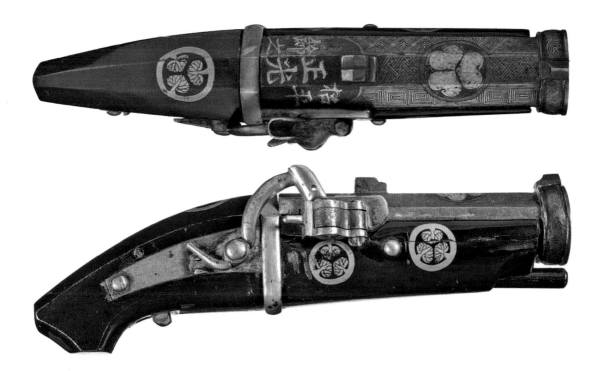

Takashina Shūhan. The *daimyō* of Nagaoka, Makino Tadayuki, an ally of the *shōgun*, had at least 2,000 breech-loading rifles acquired in the early 1860s from a German dealer named Heinrich Schnell. In addition, the Chōshū *daimyō*, Mōri Takachika, acquired 7,500 rifle-muskets – mainly British Pattern 1853 Enfields – from Scottish-born Thomas Blake Glover, a one-time Jardine Matheson clerk who had settled first in Shanghai and then in Nagasaki to found his own trading company. In 1866, 30,000 obsolescent Dreyse needle-guns were ordered, and the French, apparently at the behest of Napoleon III and seeking to secure military influence in the face of British competition, provided Tokugawa Yoshinobu – the last *shōgun* of the Tokugawa shogunate – with 2,000 new Chassepot rifles to equip his personal guard. Imperial troops mainly used Minié expanding-ball rifles such as the Enfield, which were much more accurate, lethal, and had a much longer range than the imported smoothbore muskets.

Chōshū troops are known to have used Snider breech-loaders, capable of firing ten shots a minute, against the shogunate's Shōgitai regiment at the battle of Ueno on July 4, 1868. Others were sold to men of individual *daimyō* serving the Tosa family at Ueno, for example. In the second half of the Boshin War, Tosa troops used Spencer repeating rifles and US-made handguns such as the .32 Smith & Wesson Army No. 2 revolver. Some of the latter were imported by Glover and used by Satsuma forces.

The Boshin War ended in an Imperial victory, but at least 69,000 men had been mobilized and casualties had been high. The long-established policy of expelling foreigners to protect Japan's heritage was abandoned. International trade was actively encouraged as part of a much-needed

Pistol-like *tanegashima* were also known as *bajotsutsu* ("horseback pistol"). This good-quality example, probably dating from the mid-19th century, displays the encircled *aoi mon* or crest of the Tokugawa *daimyō* – generally identified as hollyhock but actually representing wild ginger – together with what may be the *mon* of the Tokugawa-affiliated Mitusba family. Ideographs on the barrel revealing three personal names may give a clue as to this pistol's history. (Rock Island Auction, www. rockislandauction.com)

ABOVE LEFT
A first-class marksman and student of small-arms design, Murata Tsuneyoshi obtained examples of the Gras and Beaumont rifles, which formed the basis of the 11mm Meiji 13th Year Type, the IJA's first Japanese-made rifle. Murata subsequently developed the 8mm Meiji 22nd Year Type tube-magazine repeater (1889). (Author's archives)

ABOVE CENTRE
Appointed to Tōkyō Artillery Arsenal by Murata in 1891, Arisaka Nariakira developed a more sophisticated smallbore box-magazine design, the Meiji 30th Year Type rifle of 1897; it was to be the cornerstone of a progression in Japanese rifle design that lasted until the end of World War II. (Author's archives)

ABOVE RIGHT
Nambu Kijirō was inspired by Arisaka, being employed in the Koishikawa factory at the time the Meiji 30th Year Type rifle was being perfected. Nambu became part of a design-team responsible for the 9mm Meiji 26th Year Type revolver, a break-open design clearly inspired by European prototypes. (Author's archives)

modernization program. By the time of the Satsuma Rebellion of 1877, the garrisons of Tōkyō and Kumamoto were armed largely with ex-British Enfields and Sniders. Imperial forces also carried large numbers of Sniders, together with Colt and Smith & Wesson handguns (cap-locks among them), French Chassepot and German Mauser single-shot bolt-action rifles, and a few Model 1873 Winchester repeaters.

A variety of cap-lock Colt revolvers, principally the .36 Navy Model of 1851, served during the Boshin War and the Satsuma Rebellion alongside several types of Smith & Wesson cartridge revolvers. Inspiration for the purchase of these handguns lay in the cooperation treaty signed in 1858 between Japan and the United States, and the subsequent creation of agencies in Yokohama and other major Japanese cities to promote sales. Smith & Wessons had become particularly popular in the 1860s, and the .44 Russian Model was accepted as the standard handgun of the newly created Imperial Japanese Navy (IJN). Known acquisitions in 1878–1908 amounted to at least 10,000, from H. Ahrens & Co. of Yokohama (confined to 1878–79) and then Takata & Co. of Yokohama. Takata initially supplied 277 handguns, shipped from the United States on April 17, 1884, the liaison ending with 135 shipped on May 15, 1908.

Once the Meiji Era (1868–1912) had begun, the imperial authorities realized that the formation of a national army was a priority. They were also well aware that relying on imported weapons was undesirable and so embarked on the creation of suitable manufacturing facilities. The Imperial Japanese Army (IJA) Tōkyō Artillery Arsenal (*Nippon Teikoku Rikugun Tōkyō Hōheikōshō*) was opened in 1871 in the Koishikawa district and is, therefore, often represented as Koishikawa Arsenal (*Koishikawa Kōshō*). The first rifle to be manufactured in the factory – which was officially renamed "Tōkyō Army Arsenal" in April 1923 – was the 11mm Meiji 13th Year Type single-shot Murata adopted in 1880, followed in 1885 by a minor improvement of the basic design, and then in 1889 by the 8mm Meiji 22nd Year Type tube-magazine

A NOTE ON TERMINOLOGY

The designation of Nambu pistols has been the subject of great debate, largely because almost no confirmation has been found in contemporaneous Japanese sources. Consequently, the Japanese government called the perfected model, now widely known as the Model 1904 or Model 1914, little other than *Nambu Shiki Kenju*, or "Nambu Type Pistol." Although the Japanese government is said to have allowed purchase by Imperial Japanese Army (IJA) officers in 1904, IJA enlisted men armed with a handgun were still being issued with the Meiji 26th Year Type revolver.

A *Riku Shiki* ("Army Type") mark was added to the frame of handguns – perhaps after the 1909 exhibition in Toyama as a promotional aid – and the same designation was used by the Imperial Japanese Navy (IJN) when the pistol was officially adopted in 1915. Yet collectors still apply the terms "Grandpa," "Papa," and "Baby" to distinguish the major variants. In the absence of anything definitive, these terms undoubtedly still have some validity.

The 8mm "Grandpa" Nambu, the largest of the three, may date from as early as 1902. It gave way to the "improved" or "Papa"

Nambu, slightly smaller overall, and was then supplemented by the 7mm "Baby" Nambu, which was seen as an officers' model to be acquired commercially.

Another problem arises from the fact that Japanese is read from right to left, and that *Nambu Shiki* should be rendered in English as "Type Nambu" rather than "Nambu Type." Methods of transliteration have been subject to occasional changes, and "Nanbu" is now sometimes preferred to "Nambu," the style used in this study. Accented characters (e.g. "Tōkyō" instead of "Tokyo") have been used as they guide pronunciation of place and personal names.

Dates are generally given in both Western and Japanese *nengō* (regnal period) calendar systems. In addition, the Japanese used an absolute scale commencing with the mythical Jimmu *nengō*, beginning with the accession of Emperor Jimmu (r. 660–585 BC), the first emperor of Japan. Consequently, the Western year 1934 was also considered to be Year 2594, thus explaining the Type 94 pistol's designation.

repeater. One 1893 report suggested daily output of 200 rifles and 200,000 cartridges.

The large-caliber Smith & Wessons served for many years, at least one surviving to be surrendered in 1945. Mindful of the need to create an indigenous handgun design that would help Japan become less reliant on imports, however, the Japanese military authorities, still reliant on first-generation cartridge revolvers, entrusted a commission to develop a new indigenous handgun.

Numbered 2500, this distinctively marked .44 Smith & Wesson No. 3 Russian Model single-action revolver was one of those supplied to Japan in the 1870s. What may be a trademark lies on the barrel behind the maker's mark. (Morphy Auctions, www.morphyauctions.com)

DEVELOPMENT
The rise of the Nambu

While this study is primarily about the semi-automatic pistols developed by Nambu Kijirō and others and fielded by Japanese forces before and during World War II, the indigenously designed 26th Year Type revolver also deserves scrutiny, as it remained in front-line service through to 1945 and beyond alongside the semi-automatic pistols.

Approved in 1894, the new Japanese handgun (*Nijuroku-nenshiki kenju*) was a break-open revolver inspired not only by the existing Smith & Wessons but also by leading European designs such as the Mauser "Zig-Zag," the Austro-Hungarian Gasser, and the British Webley. Capable only of double-action, the 26th Year Type revolver chambered a 9×22mm rimmed cartridge offering the comparatively low power – muzzle velocity of the 150-grain bullet was only about 740ft/sec – that suited smaller-statured soldiers. One of the best features was auto-ejection, but the chambers were recessed to receive the cartridge rims and a plate on the left side of the frame could be swung out and back to expose the mechanism for maintenance once the trigger guard had been pulled down and forward. The cylinder stop was a bad design, however, as the cylinder was locked only during the cocking stroke and when the hammer was held on the sear. After firing, the cylinder could rotate freely and could theoretically place an empty chamber in line with the barrel.

It is believed that a pre-series of 250–300 26th Year Type revolvers was produced in 1893–94, lacking external marks, but series production followed, with serial numbers running as high as 59000. A "final run" then produced a few hundred revolvers with rust-blue finish and grooved grips, but large numbers of refurbished examples, the so-called "Arsenal Reworks," will also be found as the 26th Year Type survived to serve in World War II in surprising numbers. These revolvers were often accompanied by "last ditch" canvas-bodied holsters.

OPPOSITE

This 26th Year Type revolver, 54611, was manufactured in Tōkyō Artillery Arsenal at the very end of the 19th century. The pistol is 9.09in long, with a 4.72in barrel, and weighs about 1lb 15oz. Standard examples such as this one, offering exceptional charcoal-blue finish and checkered wooden grips, bore the four-circle mark of Tōkyō Artillery Arsenal, representing a pile of cannonballs, on the right side of the frame behind the cylinder and above the designation and serial number as high as 59183. Many components bear the last three digits of the serial number, and inspectors' marks will be found in various locations including the butt cap. (Morphy Auctions, www.morphyauctions.com)

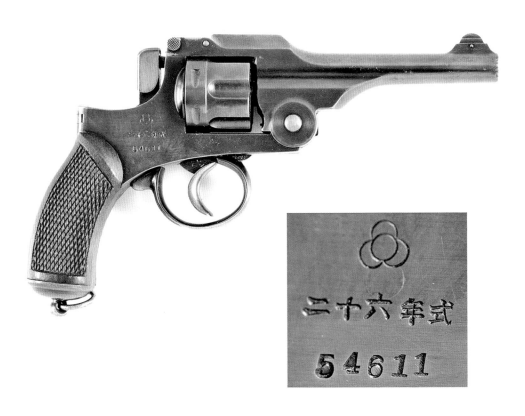

ORIGINS OF THE NAMBU

Many explanations have been offered in recent years as to the origins of the Nambu pistol. For example, Anthony Taylerson (1970: 104) suggested that the Nambu derived from the handgun designed by the Swiss "Hänsler & Roch" in the early years of the 20th century, and links between the Italian Glisenti pistol and the Nambu pistol have been claimed.

Paul Häussler and Pierre Roch, of La Chaux-de-Fonds, Neuchâtel, Switzerland, patented their invention on March 24, 1903, and the papers of Swiss patent 28228 show a recoil-operated locked breech pistol locked by a pivoting block of what Robert Wilson (n.d.: 429) calls the "propped-up" type. The locking unit lies in the rear of the frame, behind the magazine well, and is cammed into and out of engagement with the breechblock as the barrel/receiver group recoils.

Conceived at a time when the German 7.65mm Parabellum had just been adopted as the Swiss Army pistol, it is scarcely surprising that the lines of a potential competitor or replacement should be similar; and the Häussler-Roch-Pistole is no exception. Military trials may have been undertaken in 1903–04, as Taylerson suggests, but there was little chance that the Häussler-Roch-Pistole would replace the Parabellum that had been adopted for the Swiss Army in 1900. The trigger-and-sear mechanism, the jacketed barrel, and the design and position of the recoil spring (the enclosure of which contributed to the excessive action length) were all potential weaknesses.

There is evidence, however, that the Italian *Carabinieri* (Military Police) ordered some Häussler-Roch pistols for trials, though whether they were delivered is another matter. Ultimately, in 1905, an Italian military commission was charged with creating a serviceable handgun for the Italian Army on the basis of the Häussler-Roch-Pistole. Now sometimes mistakenly credited to Alfredo Glisenti personally, the transformation was undertaken by Abiel Bethel Revelli di Beaumont. Protection was sought in the name of Società Siderugica Glisenti in Italy on June 30, 1905, comparable patents being granted in Spain on April 1, 1906, in France on October 31, 1906, and in Britain on November 8, 1906 (14327/06).

Patented in 1905, the Revelli-designed Glisenti originally chambered a 7.65×22mm cartridge, but the Italian Army wanted something similar to the German 9mm Parabellum round and so the 7.65mm M1906 Glisenti became the 9mm M1910. The detachable sideplate that gave access to the action weakened the left side of the frame, meaning the 9mm Glisenti cartridge was appreciably less powerful than the 9mm Parabellum. The M1910 was adopted for Italian military service in 1910, but was never entirely satisfactory even though production continued until the blowback Beretta was adopted in 1915. An improved "Glisenti M1912" was rejected by the Italian Army and only a few had been sold commercially when World War I brought work to an end.

Sectional drawings show that the original Glisenti locking system is not sufficiently similar to the Häussler-Roch type to be hailed as a direct derivation. In addition, the locking system of the Nambu pistol bears a closer relationship to the Häussler-Roch-Pistole than the Glisenti and, consequently, it is very difficult to state categorically either that Nambu

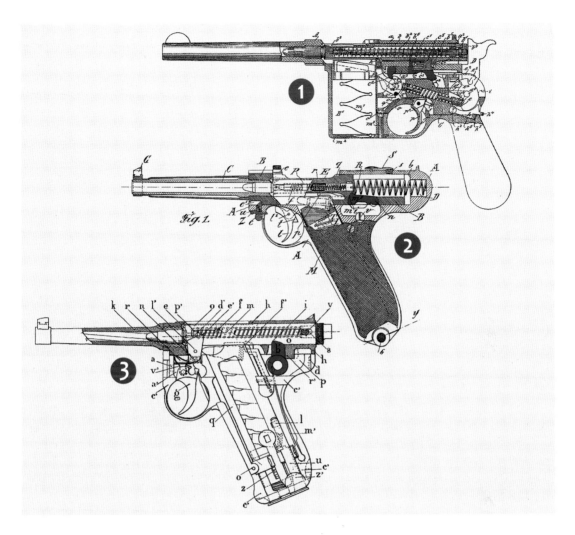

Kijirō copied the Glisenti or that the designers of the Glisenti copied the Nambu. The most likely source of inspiration of all three pistols is clearly the Mauser C/96, designed by the Feederle brothers (Fidel, Friedrich, and Josef) and patented in Germany in 1895.

As a Japanese military commission had visited the Mauser factory in Oberndorf, Germany, at a time when development of what became the Meiji 30th Year Type Arisaka rifle was beginning, it takes no great stretch of the imagination to assume that Nambu Kijirō had obtained information about the Feederle brothers' design that he then put to good use in what has even been called the "30th Year Pistol project": this would date the commencement of work to 1897.

Nambu may also have been aware of the existence of the Parabellum or Luger pistol, patented in Germany in 1898. The Nambu is shaped like the Luger, and balances far better than the C/96. In addition, early-production Lugers may have been taken to East Asia at the time of the Boxer Rebellion (1900–01) by officers serving in the Ostasiatisches Expeditionskorps and were certainly to be seen in the German Kiautshou protectorate shortly afterward.

Drawings from patents protecting the Mauser (**1**; Germany, 1895), the Häussler-Roch-Pistole (**2**; Switzerland, 1903), and the Glisenti (**3**; Britain, 1906) pistols show the locking systems of each design highlighted in red. Note how the locking blocks of the Mauser and the Häussler-Roch designs move back and down as the action recoils, but that the Glisenti block moves radially. Consequently, Nambu Kijirō's original design bears a much closer relationship to the Mauser C/96 – widely regarded as its inspiration – than the Glisenti. (Author's archives)

THE TYPE A ("GRANDPA") NAMBU

Noting that Nambu Kijirō was a field-grade officer of the IJA – i.e. ranking above major – John Moss asserts (1975: 69–70) that the pistol bearing Nambu's name must have been available prior to 1904 in order for the Japanese military authorities to authorize its purchase by officers in that year, going on to claim that it could have been in existence as early as 1899. Yet the 8mm Nambu pistol (*Nanbu kōkata jidōkenju*), subsequently known as the "Grandpa," in its finalized form seems unlikely to date as early as 1899, though prototypes may have been made. Though the design of the Nambu pistol is better than the Italian Glisenti pistols of 1906 and 1910 in many respects, whether it is representative of the late 19th century can be debated. If it had been perfected in the last years of the 19th century, however, Nambu Kijirō should rank among such luminaries as Georg Luger, Ferdinand von Mannlicher, Peter Paul Mauser, and John Moses Browning.

It is not clear whether Nambu Kijirō was a member of any purchasing and observing missions sent to Europe – in particular, when the Japanese were negotiating an agreement to license-manufacture Hotchkiss machine guns that was apparently concluded between the end of the Russo-Japanese War in May 1905 and the signing of the Treaty of Portsmouth that September. What is known, however, is that, in 1903, Arisaka Nariakira was made head of the Army Technical Bureau to refine the 30th Year Type rifle and Nambu, who had been working for some years at Tōkyō Artillery Arsenal, became chief designer on the project. It takes little stretch of the imagination to assume that when ordered to develop an auto-loading pistol to replace the 26th Year Type revolver, Nambu's first consideration would have been to analyze work being taken elsewhere. He would undoubtedly have been acquainted with some of the earliest European designs that had appeared in East Asia, such as the Mauser C/96, and, like everyone else involved in handgun design at this time, would have studied periodicals such as the Austrian *Danzer's Armee-Zeitung* and the Belgian *Revue de l'Armée Belge* in detail.

A view of Tōkyō Artillery Arsenal, Koishikawa, taken from a postcard published shortly before the Great Kantō earthquake, which seriously damaged the factory on September 1, 1923. (Author's archives)

THE HINO-KOMURO PISTOL

This remarkable pistol was designed by IJA officer Hino Kumozō and businessman Komuro Tomojirō. Application for protection was made in Japan on December 7, 1903, Japanese patent 7165 being duly granted on March 5, 1904. In addition, British patent 5,284/07 was granted on May 30, 1907, to patent agent Charles Arthur Allison of Chancery Lane, London, acting on communication from "Tomojiro Komuro, of Ushigome, Tōkyō, in the Empire of Japan, Manufacturer." US patent 886211, sought on September 23, 1904, was granted on April 28, 1908.

Perhaps as many as 500 Hino-Komuro pistols were produced in Komuro's firearms factory in the Toyotama district of Tōkyō, from 1904 until possibly 1912. Chambered for the 7.65mm Browning (.32 ACP) cartridge, a typical example, pistol 69, was 9.33in long with a 7.64in barrel and weighed 1lb 13oz. Changes were made, however, to what were largely hand-made products as time passed: for example, the magazine and loading system was modified; and the markings were usually confined to an encircled "ko" trademark and an acknowledgment of Japanese Patent 7165.

A Komuro catalogue dating from c.1908 claims that the Hino-Komuro pistols could be chambered for any cartridge in the 5–8mm bracket, with magazines of 8–15 rounds, but only two non-7.65mm examples have been found. Chambered for the 8mm Nambu cartridge, Hino-Komuro pistol 184 is reportedly 10.43in overall, has an 8.54in barrel, and weighs approximately 2lb.

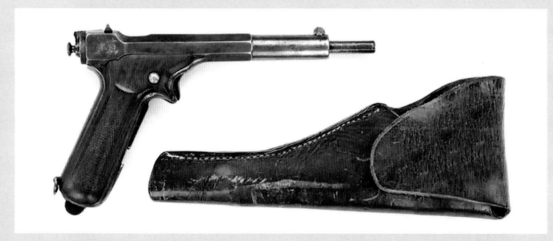

Hino-Komuro pistol 435 with its holster. One of very few examples chambered for an 8mm cartridge, this pistol has an eight-round magazine with the catch on the base of the front grip – where it can easily be released accidentally. This pistol was surrendered in China in 1945 to a sailor from a US Navy minesweeper. (Morphy Auctions, www.morphyauctions.com)

Sometimes claimed to have been known as "Meiji 35th Year Type," but with no real evidence, the Nambu pistol is often said to have been perfected in 1902 and tested by the IJA in 1904. Although adoption was not recommended, possibly on the grounds of cost, approval was given for Japanese officers – who were required to provide their own personal weapons – to purchase the pistols individually.

A report from the British military attaché in Tōkyō claimed that the first public exhibition of the Nambu pistol occurred at the graduation ceremony of the Toyama Military Academy in June 1909, and no contemporaneous Japanese source has yet been found to refer to an introduction date as early as 1904. Nothing among the dispatches and reports from the Russo-Japanese War suggests that Japanese troops were carrying anything other than 26th Year Type revolvers introduced in 1893. Officers' weapons such as the Mauser C/96 were used in small quantities, however, and a few "Grandpa" Nambu pistols may have been among them.

About 2,500 "Grandpa" Nambu pistols are believed to have been made in 1903–06, with observed serial numbers ranging from 3 to 2354. Bearing the four-circle mark of Tōkyō Artillery Arsenal, they accepted an eight-round magazine. No significant variations have been identified, though there are two types of shoulder stock. In addition to the sales to military personnel that were undoubtedly made privately, it has been estimated that 350 "Grandpa" pistols, accompanied by shoulder stocks, went to Thailand early in the 20th century; these invariably display a *chakra*, "war-quoit," marking.

THE PERFECTED TYPE A ("PAPA") NAMBU

The original "Grandpa" Nambu pistol had soon been improved, creating the so-called "Papa" version that was then adopted by the IJN in 1915. Though the "Grandpa" and "Papa" patterns are essentially the same and of similar dimensions, the "Grandpa" has a round-edged trigger lever inside a noticeably tiny trigger guard. A safety blade is let into the front grip-strap, and a tangent-leaf sight lies on top of the receiver. A stock-attachment slot is milled into the back-strap and a fixed lanyard loop projects backward below the cocking knob. Attaching lanyards was encouraged in service to avoid losing pistols unnecessarily.

The material and blued finish was usually exemplary, but only about 2,500 "Grandpa" Nambu pistols had been produced before several improvements – generally minor – led to the "Papa" variant. The trigger guard was enlarged to admit a gloved finger, the trigger lever was square-edged instead of rounded, the tangent-leaf sight was reduced in size, and a cast-alloy magazine base replaced the vulnerable wooden version. Then came the IJN variant, adopted in 1915, manufactured initially by Tōkyō

THE NAMBU REVEALED

8mm "Papa" variant, 1902

Nambu pistols are striker-fired and have an extraordinary sear bar extending to the rear of the mechanism, though the sear itself is a very clever design with a simple and positive spring-loaded disconnector plunger attached to its nose. The trigger lifts the sear as it rotates and disengages the firing pin; but when the barrel and receiver recoil, a small lug on the underside of the barrel pushes the plunger backward to disconnect it from the trigger. The sear then springs down to its original position, from which it cannot be lifted until the removal of finger pressure allows the trigger-nose to slip back under the plunger.

The trigger assembly slides in dovetailed grooves cut in the front grip-strap and carries the only manual safety, an odd spring-loaded lever that intercepts the trigger. The trigger and safety assemblies are theoretically interchangeable. It is notable that the original Nambu pistol has neither manual nor magazine safeties, unlike the later Taishō 14th Year Type, which has both.

The barrel/barrel extension unit (**2**) reciprocates within the frame and the bolt (**5**) moves within the barrel extension. A lug on the top of the locking block (**13**), pivoting around a concave-faced block under the receiver, engages a recess in the underside of the bolt to lock the mechanism.

When the pistol is fired, barrel and barrel extension recoil through about 0.2in, relying on a rod attached to the cocking piece (**11**) to compress the recoil spring (**6**) that lies in a longitudinal tunnel in the left side of the frame. The tail of the locking block then drops from its plateau to release the bolt. The barrel and barrel extension stop against a lug on top of the trigger-guard unit (**23**), freeing the bolt to run back alone and then return under pressure from the recoil spring.

The firing pin (**7**), held back on the sear (**15**) under pressure from the firing-pin spring (**8**), can be released to fire again simply by pressing the trigger (**25**) if the grip-safety lever (**20**) is also being depressed.

1. Front sight
2. Barrel
3. Cartridge in chamber
4. Extractor
5. Bolt
6. Recoil spring (shown separately)
7. Firing pin
8. Firing-pin spring
9. Bolt lock/striker-spring guide
10. Adjustable rear sight
11. Cocking knob
12. Lanyard loop
13. Locking block
14. Locking-block spring
15. Sear
16. Cartridges in magazine
17. Magazine base
18. Magazine spring
19. Magazine follower
20. Grip-safety lever
21. Grip
22. Magazine catch
23. Trigger guard
24. Trigger and grip-safety spring
25. Trigger
26. Sear bar plunger spring
27. Sear bar plunger

Artillery Arsenal and then by Tōkyō Gasu Denki (TGE, "Tokyo Gas & Electric"). These pistols customarily display anchor marks. TGE products generally lack the stock slot in the butt-heel and have one-piece frames lacking the milled-out panel behind the grip. They also have a lanyard ring instead of a fixed loop.

It has been suggested that the IJN authorities ordered the stock slots to be filled either when the pistols were formally inventoried or when the 14th Year Type was adopted for naval service in 1929. There was little use for holster-stocks, which occupied space aboard ship that could be put to better use, and it has also been suggested that objections were raised to the sharp-edged stock slots catching on clothing.

Still chambered for the 8×22mm Nambu cartridge and retaining the eight-round magazine, the perfected Type A Nambu pistol (*Nanbu kōkata jidō kenju*), known as the "Papa" Nambu, was much the same length as the "Grandpa" version, and its 4.69in barrel retained the previous pistol's six-groove right-hand-twist rifling. Weight was about 2lb 2oz. Several variations were manufactured by Tōkyō Artillery Arsenal and, at a later date, by Tōkyō Gasu Denki Kabushiki Kaisha (TGE, "Tōkyō Gas & Electric Company," later known simply as "Gasuden").

Tōkyō-made pistols came in two basic types. The standard version had a one-piece frame with milled-out panels behind the grip, and generally lacked the stock slot cut into the heel of the butt. Running-on from the "Grandpa" pistols, serial numbers reached at least 7050. Variants widely associated with Thailand, generally numbered in the 4550–4750 range but rarely encountered, were supplied with a shoulder stock and display a *chakra* mark instead of "Army Type."

On September 10, 1909, the Nambu (*Kaigun jidōkenju shi-nenshiki*) was officially adopted by the IJN to replace aging .44 Smith & Wesson revolvers in the hands of the Special Naval Landing Forces (marines) and other naval personnel. It seems likely that an order was placed with Tōkyō Artillery Arsenal at this time. These pistols are now widely known as the "4th Year Type." The fourth year of the Taishō *nengō* fell not in 1909,

NAMBU MARKINGS

Kanji ideographs denoting "Nambu Type" (式部南, *Nambu Shiki*) appear on the right side of all frames, while "Army Type" (式陸, *Riku Shiki*) may be found on the left side of many. There is no evidence that any pistols were officially purchased – other than for the IJN – and the *Riku Shiki* inscription may have been little more than a sales gimmick, as most contemporary Japanese service weapons such as the 26th Year Type revolver, rifles, machine guns, and mortars display a *nengō* designation; and so the absence of this on the Nambu pistols, in spite of its inclusion in some official training manuals, precludes official adoption.

Tōkyō Artillery Arsenal relied on the well-established four-cannonball mark, while the Tōkyō Gas & Electric Industry Company (東京瓦斯電気工業), known as TGE, applied an encircled "GTE" mark in which the letter "T" was dominant. John Moss (1975: 71–72) speculated that what he termed "Arabic" letters are unlikely to relate to a transliteration of the manufacturer's name into English, but his interpretation has been questioned. Founded in 1912 after merging with the Chiyoda Gas Company, TGE was simply seeking to sell its products internationally under a trademark which may have been inspired by General Electric Company's well-established encircled "GE" accepted in the United States on July 24, 1899.

In addition, Nambu pistols bore serial numbers represented in Arabic numerals despite the existence of *kanji* numerals (which were widely used prior to 1900): further evidence that indigenous and Western languages were often intermixed.

A composite view of IJN-marked TGE-made Nambu 2683, and its clamshell-type holster fitted with a shoulder strap. An anchor mark accompanies *Nambu Shiki* and the serial number on the right side of the receiver, while the left side displays *Riku Shiki*. The manufacturer's identifier lies above the chamber, and "23" (in *kanji* characters) is on the grip. (Rock Island Auction, www.rockislandauction.com)

however, but in 1915, at a time when the Japanese were embroiled, albeit in limited fashion, in World War I. Consequently, it is possible that "Taishō 4th Year Type" referred specifically to the contract for "Army Type" Nambu pistols placed by the IJN authorities with TGE at a time when the production capacity of Tōkyō Artillery Arsenal was insufficient.

Collectors now recognize ten subvariants of the "Papa" Nambu, two made at Tōkyō Artillery Arsenal and eight by TGE: one of the most

Tōkyō-made "Papa" Nambu 8796 embodies a later one-piece frame design with a panel milled-out behind the grip. The pistol is marked *Nambu Shiki* above the serial number on the right side of the receiver, and *Riku Shiki* ("Army Type") on the left side. The four-circle Tōkyō Artillery Arsenal mark lies above the chamber, and the number "20" and what may be a personal name have been painted on the grip. The typically optimistic tangent back sight, graduated from 100m to 500m (109–547yd), was too complicated for a service handgun the effective range of which scarcely exceeded 50m (55yd). (Rock Island Auction, www.rockislandauction.com)

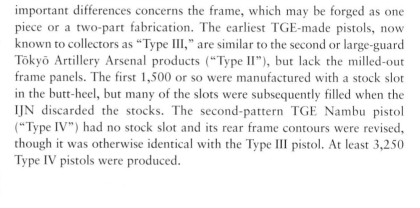

Found on "Baby" Nambu 4675, the *kanji* inscription *on-shi* is an abbreviated form of "meritorious gift." Some "Baby" Nambu pistols can be found bearing presentation inscriptions from officials of high rank – even, in a few cases, from the emperor himself – while others were given as prizes by the military academies. Currently, only 14 pistols of this type are known to survive. (Amoskeag Auctions, www.amoskeagauction.com)

important differences concerns the frame, which may be forged as one piece or a two-part fabrication. The earliest TGE-made pistols, now known to collectors as "Type III," are similar to the second or large-guard Tōkyō Artillery Arsenal products ("Type II"), but lack the milled-out frame panels. The first 1,500 or so were manufactured with a stock slot in the butt-heel, but many of the slots were subsequently filled when the IJN discarded the stocks. The second-pattern TGE Nambu pistol ("Type IV") had no stock slot and its rear frame contours were revised, though it was otherwise identical with the Type III pistol. At least 3,250 Type IV pistols were produced.

THE TYPE B ("BABY") NAMBU

Very little is known about the history of the Type B Nambu pistol (*Nanbu otsukata jidōkenju*). Often called the "Baby" Nambu by modern commentators to distinguish it from the larger service ("Papa") type, it was designated the Type B in Japanese service to distinguish it from the Type A pistol. The "Baby" Nambu existed only in rumor until some were captured during the Pacific campaigns of 1941–45. Firearms expert Julian S. Hatcher had supplied a few details of the pistol to US Army intelligence during the 1930s but, as Frederick Leithe notes (1967), some doubted its very existence while others found the prospect laughable. Many authorities simply refused to believe in a tiny locked-breech handgun that fired such a small cartridge, even though many European staff officers favored blowbacks chambering the 6.35mm Auto (.25 ACP) round.

Made of good-quality material and largely hand-finished, the tiny 7mm-caliber "Baby" Nambu pistols are mechanically identical with the standard 8mm pattern, although components are suitably reduced in size and magazine capacity is reduced from eight rounds to seven. They share

recoil operation with their larger predecessors, rely on the same propped-up lug beneath the bolt to lock the action, and the sear bar has the same special plunger-type disconnector. A mere 6.97in long, with a 3.27in barrel rifled with six-groove right-hand-twist rifling, the pistol weighs about 1lb 5oz. The plain-bordered grips and fixed-notch back sight are also most distinctive.

The 7×20mm cartridge was more powerful than the widely distributed 6.35mm Auto (.25 ACP), but muzzle energy was still comparatively low. Consequently, the "Baby" Nambu could easily have been a cheaper and simpler blowback than the standard locked-breech 8mm Nambu, which was complicated and therefore expensive to manufacture. Two "Baby" Nambu pistols combined with the blade of a *tanto* (short sword) survive, one in the Aberdeen Proving Ground Collection, but there is no evidence that any more than a handful were made.

Most of the surviving "Baby" Nambu pistols bear the four-circle Tōkyō Artillery Arsenal mark over the chamber, although a few display the TGE logo. They are probably contemporary with the "Papa" Nambu pistol and the first TGE pattern. Total production has been estimated as 5,900 by Tōkyō Artillery Arsenal, beginning early in the 20th century and ending when the factory was damaged by the Great Kantō earthquake on September 1, 1923, and then perhaps only 550 by TGE from 1923 until the end of the decade. Serial-number ranges are currently recorded as 46–5881 and 5902–6443 respectively, some of the earliest pistols, Tōkyō and TGE alike, incorporating minor manufacturing variations testifying to their preproduction status.

Two views of "Baby" Nambu 5568. "Baby" Nambu pistols were intended to be purchased privately by IJA officers. The recipients had no need of large-caliber combat weapons but, mindful of the reactionary splinter groups within the armed forces, doubtless valued a means of personal protection. Many have survived in good condition, as they had been meticulously cleaned and cared for by orderlies – in contrast to the cavalier treatment of service weapons. (Rock Island Auction, www.rockislandauction.com)

As with many countries' armed forces, the Japanese military issued handguns to NCOs and enlisted men serving in specialist arms of service such as the cavalry and the artillery. Here, a Japanese artilleryman, apparently ranking as superior private, poses with an antiquated breech-loading cannon. A Nambu holster suspended from a shoulder strap lies on his right hip, while the lanyard attached to the pistol runs around his neck and under his shoulder. (Author's archives)

THE 14TH YEAR TYPE PISTOL

The Japanese armed forces became keen to adopt a semi-automatic pistol after World War I ended, but were aware that the Type A Nambu was too complicated to be mass-produced sufficiently cheaply. The mid-1920s proved a convenient time to select a new design as the Great Kantō earthquake had destroyed the original Nambu production line, and retooling was consequently essential. A new pistol was developed in Tōkyō Army Arsenal by a military commission, with which Nambu Kijirō was undoubtedly involved in a consultant's role – his had been the original design, after all, and he was acknowledged as Japan's leading small-arms expert.

The result of work completed in 1925 was the Taishō 14th Year Type pistol (*Taishō jidōkenjū juyon-nenshiki*); 1925 being the 14th year of the *nengō*. Manufacture was entrusted to the IJA arsenals in Nagoya-Chigusa and Tōkyō, the former completing its first pistols in November 1926 (Taishō 15.11) and the latter in May 1928. Emperor Yoshihito died on December 25, 1926, and his successor, Hirohito, named his *nengō* "Enlightening Peace" or *Shōwa*. Consequently, the first Tōkyō-made pistols were date-marked "Shōwa 3.5." They were 9.09in long, had 4.61in barrels with the standard six-groove right-hand-twist rifling, and weighed about 2lb 3oz; magazines held eight 8×22mm rounds.

The committee simplified the mechanism of the original Nambu pistol, but as the Japanese lacked widespread experience of handgun design, the 14th Year Type pistol was unnecessarily complicated and only moderately efficient. The design of the 14th Year Type components permitted quicker and easier production, as fine manufacturing tolerances were no longer necessary. The Nambu frame was simplified so that it bridged the receiver only at the rear, where it supported the V-notch back sight, and the asymmetrical bolt-return-spring chamber was eliminated. The sides of the 14th Year Type receiver were flat. The barrel and receiver, forged and machined in a single piece as those of the old Nambu had been, reflected the continuing influence of Mauser C/96 pistols captured during the Russo-Japanese War.

The shape and machining of the locking piece were greatly revised, though it remained a separate propped-up block beneath the rear of the receiver (where it engaged a recess in the bolt). The circular transverse tip of the locking-piece shaft passed between the sides of the bifurcated receiver block, however, unlike the original Nambu pistol in which a hollow locking unit engaged a solid receiver block.

One inexplicably bad feature of the 14th Year Type pistol is the absence of a separate mechanical hold-open. The magazine follower keeps the bolt back after the last round has been chambered, fired, and ejected. Other handgun designers had previously experimented with this system, but it was universally agreed to be inefficient. Pressure from a powerful mainspring often makes it difficult to withdraw the magazine; and the breech closes when the magazine is removed so that the slide must be retracted to load the first new cartridge. The former is especially notable in the 14th Year Type, the double mainsprings of which were reinforced after 1940 by an auxiliary magazine spring on the lower front of the grip.

14TH YEAR TYPE SAFETY FEATURES

The tail of the firing pin protruded below the bolt instead of from the left side, and the sear and disconnector system was altered. A lug on the trigger – replacing the spring-loaded disconnector plunger on the tip of the Nambu sear bar – acted in conjunction with the receiver stop-lug to prevent the trigger meshing with the sear until the breech was reloaded and the trigger released. The spring-loaded sear consisted of a simple bar with its tip bent through 90 degrees to pass under the bolt and engage the firing pin, and was raised by a step on the tail of the trigger. It gives a light pull, lighter than even the original Nambu pistol, although some inherent "creep" occurs because the sear nose has to move vertically to release the firing pin.

Unfortunately, no mechanical safety mechanism was built into the trigger unit, and the disconnector only ensures that the trigger and sear bar do not mesh during the reloading cycle. As a result, the firing pin could be jarred out of engagement with the sear bar by the shock of the bolt hitting the breech face and a loaded pistol will fire. This normally happens only in pistols in which the sear-to-firing pin contact is insufficient, however.

The grip safety of the "Papa" Nambu, which had blocked the trigger until it was squeezed (not always infallibly), was replaced by a multipurpose lever-operated device on the left side of the frame above the trigger aperture. The pistol could be fired when the lever was pushed upward and forward through 180 degrees, to point to 火 (hi, "fire"); rotating the lever backward to 安 (an, "safe") locked the barrel/receiver group and prevented the sear from moving vertically. Finally, once the left grip was removed, the lever could be rotated downward until it could be taken out of the frame completely. The trigger subgroup, locked by the safety-lever spindle, is slid downward and the retraction grip unscrewed from the bolt – whereafter the receiver can be run forward off the frame.

The safety was efficient and effective, but could only be operated by the fingers of the non-firing hand. Better designs – such as the German Parabellum – featured safeties that could be reached by the thumb of the firing hand without having to remove the finger from the trigger or unduly disturbing aim.

14th Year Type pistols made after 1932 (Shōwa 7) also had a magazine safety. Introduced as a result of service experience in Manchuria, this took the form of a horizontally pivoted block in the top front of the magazine well. The nose of the block tilts into the well when the magazine is removed, and its tail intercepts the trigger so that the pistol cannot fire. The block rotates to disengage the block-tail from the trigger when the magazine is inserted in the feed-way and pushed fully home. The feature is, however, of dubious utility and typical of many critical reviews are:

This [the magazine safety] ... is not really a safety device at all, but a rather irritating provision to prevent the pistol being fired unless a magazine is in the butt. It is often incorporated in small pocket pistols where such a device may be of advantage as an indicator, but it is seldom found in military pistols ... being quite unnecessary in service conditions. (Wilson n.d.: 448)

Military safeties usually allow a pistol to operate even if they fail, but most "magazine" types are designed to be fail-safe – a theoretical consideration rather than a practical application. The Germans, for example, realistically discarded the fail-safe safety system of the Walther *Heeres-Pistole* before accepting the P 38 for service use, because the *Heeres-Pistole*'s hammer could not fire the weapon if the safety fractured in its applied position.

The 14th Year Type magazine is retained by a spring-loaded transverse catch that lies behind the trigger on the left side of the frame.

Robert Wilson noted that:

... it was possible in a well maintained pistol, given fairly strong fingers, to withdraw the empty magazine against the pressure exerted by the retracted bolt ... using two hands. With a dirty pistol, or if the hands are wet or greasy, this is virtually impossible. Unless assistance is forthcoming, resort to one of two courses is possible ... (i) Press down on the magazine follower with some instrument such as a thin piece of wood or a cleaning rod – withdrawing it smartly as the bolt runs forward, then remove the magazine in the normal manner. This method is by no means as easy as it sounds. (ii) Grasp the pistol firmly in the left hand, butt uppermost, using a finger to press in the magazine catch; with the right hand, retract the bolt slightly and pull out the magazine with the teeth ... (Wilson n.d.: 454–55)

THE 14TH YEAR TYPE EXPOSED

8mm pre-1940 "small guard" version

The barrel and barrel extension (**2**) run back within the frame (**24**) until their travel is stopped by a vertical blade on the trigger lever (**27**), whereupon the bolt (**5**) separates from the propped-up locking block (**15**) and continues backward within the barrel extension. Recoil springs (**6**) lie on each side of the bolt in specially machined channels, to control recoil and the bolt-return stroke by bearing against lugs on the frame. The recoil springs work efficiently despite the lack of guides or pins, as they are supported by the bolt body and the walls of the barrel extension. At the end of the recoil stroke, the springs return the barrel and barrel extension to their initial position, pushing a new cartridge forward out of the magazine (**18**) into the chamber (**3**), raising the locking-block lug back into engagement with the bolt, and leaving the firing pin (**7**) held back on the sear (**14**) against pressure from the firing-pin spring (**8**). Pressing the trigger (**25**) then allows another shot.

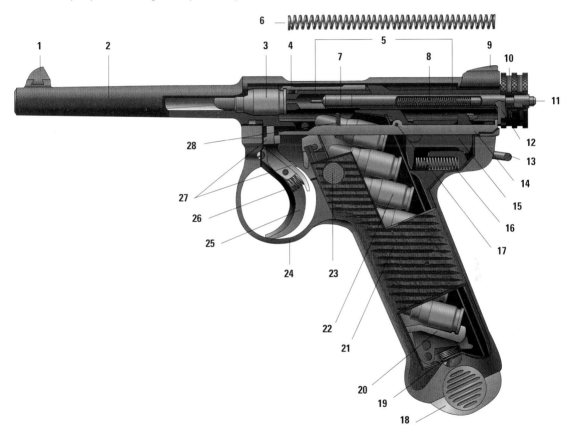

1. Front sight
2. Barrel
3. Cartridge in chamber
4. Extractor
5. Bolt
6. Recoil spring (shown separately)
7. Firing pin
8. Firing-pin spring
9. Rear sight
10. Bolt nut

11. Firing-pin guide
12. Firing-pin tail
13. Lanyard loop
14. Sear
15. Locking block
16. Locking-block spring
17. Sear pin
18. Magazine
19. Magazine spring
20. Magazine follower

21. Grip
22. Cartridges in magazine
23. Magazine catch
24. Frame/trigger guard
25. Trigger
26. Trigger spring
27. Trigger lever
28. Sear spring

This feature, in collusion with the suspect firing-pin spring, probably caused the premature demise of countless Japanese officers in close-quarter fighting. In a footnote, Wilson stated that "during the course of a minor engagement in 1945," he had encountered a

> Japanese officer struggling with a Year 14 pistol. Being too busy at the time … he returned later to retrieve this officer's pistol and sword … Subsequently, the pistol was brought in by one of the native allies who observed that the weapon was useless as the breech would not close. [The] bolt was merely retracted on an empty magazine, but [Wilson] had to have help to get the latter out, this being the first time he had encountered a Year 14 pistol. Apart from being wet and muddy the arm was in serviceable condition. The writer has no doubt that this Japanese officer felt before he died that his pistol had let him down. (Wilson n.d.: 455)

The earliest 14th Year Type pistols were made of passably good material and were generally well finished; their bluing was often equal to that of many of the best contemporary Western products. The poor components-fit, however, generally meant that even major components were rarely interchangeable and it is evident that appreciable hand finishing – in the early years as well as the later stages of World War II – was necessary on each pistol. The pistols were much more angular than their Nambu predecessors, the old asymmetric spring-housing having been discarded. The earliest 14th Year Type pistols can be found with bolt-retraction grips consisting of three separate circular milled flanges, small trigger guards, and no auxiliary magazine-retaining springs.

Judged by Western standards, output of the 14th Year Type was slow. The first pistols were completed in Nagoya Army Arsenal's Chigusa factory toward the end of 1926, little over a hundred bearing Taisho-era dates ("15.11" and "15.12" are known) as they had been completed prior to the emperor's death. A Shōwa prefix was then substituted, however, and work continued until November 1932 (Shōwa 7.11).

Production at Tōkyō Army Arsenal in Koishikawa began in May 1928. The Tōkyō facilities had been badly damaged in the Great Kantō earthquake, however, and plans to relocate arms facilities to less vulnerable areas were ratified in October 1927. Consequently, a new IJA arsenal in Kokura became operative on November 1, 1933, but the transfer of work from Tōkyō took time.

Though assembly was no longer undertaken in Tōkyō, parts including frames were still being made in November 1934 and responsibility for inspection was not transferred to Kokura until March 1935 (Shōwa 10.3). By this time, about 32,000 had been made. Although 14th Year Type pistols were assembled at Kokura until June 1936 (Shōwa 11.6), it is suspected that many of their parts had been transferred from Tōkyō Army Arsenal.

Nagoya Army Arsenal also ceased production at the end of 1932, work transferring to Nambu-Seisakusho a year later. The machinery may have been acquired by the Nambu company and installed in the Kitatama

Two views of Nambu-Seisakusho 14th Year Type pistol 12012, dating from June 1935 (Shōwa 10.6). (Amoskeag Auctions, www.amoskeagauction.com)

("Kokubunji") manufactory. The Nambu-Seisakusho business, founded by Nambu Kijirō in 1927, had moved to Tōkyō-Kitatama in 1929 and was renamed Chūō-Kōgyō Kabushiki Kaisha on December 1, 1936, after merging with Taisei Kōgyō Kabushiki Kaisha.

The original Nagoya serial-number sequence ended in November 1932 slightly above 7800, while the earliest Nambu-made 14th Year Type pistol yet discovered, 7835, is dated December 1933 (Shōwa 8.12). It seems that a pre-series, perhaps assembled largely from existing parts with marks only of Nagoya arsenal, soon gave way to standard 14th Year Type pistols with the Nambu symbol added above the Nagoya mark.

In February 1934 (Shōwa 9.2), after about 500 of these otherwise standard "small trigger guard" pistols had been made, the marks became horizontal and work continued until the advent in September 1939 (Shōwa 14.9) of the transitional large-guard pattern. About 58,000 "small guard" guns had been made by this time.

Nambu Seisakusho/Chūō-Kōgyō, which continued to make 14th Year Type pistols until August 1944 (Shōwa 19.8), seems to have been the only contractor active from 1934 until production in the Toriimatsu factory of Nagoya Army Arsenal, suspended in 1932, resumed in December 1941 (Shōwa 16.12), and continued until August 1945 (Shōwa 20.8).

THE TYPE 94 PISTOL

The bizarre appearance of the 8mm Type 94 pistol (*Kyūyon-Shiki Kenjū*), the oddest of the Japanese service pistols, has excited a great deal of controversy, but much of its developmental history remains obscure. Commentators such as Leithe (1967) have suggested that it was developed in the early 1930s to encourage exports to Central and South America, but Wilson dismisses the uncorroborated theory:

14TH YEAR TYPE AND TYPE 94 MARKINGS

Five sets of marks, sometimes accompanied by other marks, are found prefixing 14th Year Type pistols' serial numbers. Starting with **manufacturer marks**, the government arsenals in Tokyo and then Kokura used the well-established "four cannonballs" mark, while Nagoya Army Arsenal's mark was a stylized representation of two fighting fish. The initially privately operated Nambu-Seisakusho/Chūō-Kōgyō factory used the first syllable of "Nambu," adapted to become approximately circular.

Type 94 pistols usually display the Nagoya and Nambu marks on the right side of the frame, though their position varies. A small number dating from June 1935 (Shōwa 10.6) have the marks close together by the serial number. About 7,300 were then made prior to January 1939 (Shōwa 14.1), however, with the Nagoya Army Arsenal and Nambu/Chūō-Kōgyō components noticeably separated from each other; the "Nambu-Nagoya" marks were then applied below the date on about 11,750 pistols produced between January 1939 and August 1941 (Shōwa 16.8). Then came at least 22,000 with "Nagoya-Nambu" marks (August 1941 to January 1944, Shōwa 19.1) and, from Shōwa 19.1 until the end of production in June 1945 (Shōwa 20.6), 30,000 Type 94 pistols with the marks separated once again.

Turning to **designation markings**, 14th Year Type pistols have *Ju-yon nenshiki* ("14th Year Type") on the right side of the frame,

while Type 94 pistols display *Ku-yon Shiki* ("94 Type") on the left side of the frame above the trigger aperture.

There are also markings relating to the **regnal period**. The *nengō* concept relied on each emperor's reign being considered as an individual era. Consequently, the character 昭, identifying the Shōwa *nengō*, generally appears in conjunction with the date, on the right-side rear of the 14th Year Type frame. The Type 94 also displays the Shōwa mark on the right-side rear of the frame.

In terms of **date marks**, 14th Year Type pistols are dated on the right side of the frame behind the grip. Type 94 pistols' date of manufacture (or perhaps acceptance) appears on the right-side rear of the frame. Marks such as "12.7," indicating the seventh month of the 12th year of the Shōwa *nengō*, equate to July 1937.

With respect to **serial numbers**, 14th Year Type pistols are numbered on the right-side rear of the frame, where the serial number is invariably prefixed by the arsenal's trademark, while Type 94 pistols are numbered on the right side of the frame above the trigger.

The encircled characters イ and ロ will also be found, though their use was restricted to pistols manufactured in the Chūō-Kōgyō and Nagoya-Toriimatsu factories. Widely used to distinguish minor design variations among bombs, fuzes, cannon, and other military

"Large guard" 14th Year Type pistol *i*-3791, made in the Nagoya-Toriimatsu factory in December 1941 (Shōwa 16.12), displays "fire" and "safe" marks with the safety lever, while the designation lies on the rear of the slide. The magazine-retaining spring on the grip-front was added in 1940. (Amoskeag Auctions, www.amoskeagauction.com)

stores, the characters do not represent significant revisions in the context of 14th Year Type pistols, as changes of character do not correspond with the only major alterations in the pistols' construction. It has been suggested – for example, by Leithe (1967) – that these were inspectors' marks for two areas, but Leithe cites no evidence for this statement. The spread of the serial numbers, and the periods in which each of the contractors produced the pistols shows that each symbol does not represent a finite time period – a financial year, for example. Yet another theory, that the symbols represent different sub-plants of a single arsenal, can also be disregarded: the Nagoya-Toriimatsu marks run consecutively rather than concurrently, and both Nagoya-Toriimatsu and Chūō-Kōgyō share the character イ. The explanation is simply that a cyclical serial-numbering system had been adopted, blocks of 99,999 units being given a distinguishing prefix in much the same way as the Germans had done with their small arms (notably the Parabellum pistols and Mauser rifles).

The *kana* phonetic alphabet provided the basis for the prefix marks, as the simple characters made legible punches. Their sequence is widely believed to have followed the *Iroha* poem, which contains nearly 50 symbols (from *i* to *su*) without repetition. Only the first two *kana* characters, *i* (イ) and *ro* (ロ), appeared on the pistols, as none of their contractors reached the third (*ha*, ハ) and fourth (*ni*, ニ) blocks as the rifle-makers had done. In addition,

only the output of the Nagoya-Toriimatsu factory of Nagoya Army Arsenal during 1941–45 was large enough to require the use of serial-number prefixes. There are, however, three Nagoya-made 14th Year Type pistols with identical serial numbers: one is 2345, the second *i*-2345 and the third *ro*-2345.

Magazines, triggers, breechblocks, and some other major components often bear the last three digits of the serial number. This can be taken to indicate that the vital components were not totally interchangeable, as the pistols were subjected to a large amount of hand finishing.

In terms of **other marks**, firing instructions – 火 (*hi*, "fire"), and 安 (*an*, "safe") – appear alongside the 14th Year Type pistol's safety lever and on the safety-lever surround, while inspectors' marks may be found on some of the larger parts, notably the frame and the receiver. Sometimes said to identify the "head of the department of control" or "chief inspector," these marks can often be linked with the factory name or location: 小 (*ko*) for Kokura Army Arsenal, 千 (*chi*) for the Chigusa factory of Nagoya Army Arsenal, and 名 (*na*) for Nagoya Army Arsenal itself. Research into the identification of inspectors' marks is still being undertaken in great detail, by James Brown and others, as these marks can determine the origin of individual parts. Personal marks, sometimes found painted on the grips, are usually confined to numbers and names; units are rarely identified.

The frame of this Type 94 pistol displays firing instructions alongside the safety lever, with the designation *Ku-yon Shiki* ("94 Type") above the trigger aperture. The date Shōwa 17.2, February 1942, lies above the Nagoya and Nambu symbols on the right-side rear, with the serial number 23660 above the trigger. (Morphy Auctions, www.morphyauctions.com)

TYPE 94 SAFETY FEATURES

When the pistol fires, the barrel/slide assembly recoils until the barrel stop-lug strikes a cam on the front of the trigger plunger; this forces the plunger head down against its spring to disconnect the plunger (and thus the trigger) from the sear nose. The sear spring then forces the sear tail back into engagement with the hammer, but the plunger cannot re-engage the sear nose until the firer has released the trigger. This consequently takes care of disconnection and the phenomenon of trigger "clutch," which could otherwise occur when the firer rotated the trigger past the point at which the sear was released. The pistol then fires, and would continue to fire until the trigger was released if a suitable disconnection system was not included in its design.

A manual safety catch lies on the left-side rear of the frame where it can be rotated across the sear bar to lock the sear tail securely into the hammer. Simple and very effective, the safety catch can be applied by the thumb of the firing hand without unduly disturbing aim – unlike the clumsy arrangement of the earlier 14th Year Type pistol.

An exceptionally simple magazine safety is merged with the Type 94's magazine-release cross-bolt. When the magazine is removed from the feed-way, the tip of the magazine safety springs into the gap and its tail is lifted into a notch cut in the back of the trigger. Although this is a reasonably effective safety provision, the design of the sear bar – which can be

released from the hammer when its external surface is struck – makes it possible to fire the Type 94 even with the magazine removed, though this was hardly the primary function of the external sear.

The usefulness of any magazine safety is questionable, however; there can be no valid reason for its inclusion in a military weapon, regardless of its efficiency. A pistol so fitted cannot usually be fired if the magazine is lost, even though loose cartridges may be readily available.

The Type 94, just as with the Nambu and 14th Year Type pistols, lacked a mechanical hold-open. The magazine follower held the slide open after the last round had been loaded, fired, and the cartridge case ejected, though the weaker mainspring of the Type 94 made the task of withdrawing the empty magazine rather easier than it had been on the 14th Year Type. As the magazine follower was removed from contact with the breechblock, the slide ran forward onto an empty chamber.

When a fresh magazine was inserted in the feed-way and pushed home, the slide had to be manually retracted and returned to cock and load. The slides of many other military pistols were held open by catches, springs or levers until the new magazine was inserted, whereafter tripping a button or lever allowed the slide to run forward: this eliminated the manual retraction stroke and saved time.

It was adopted into the Imperial Japanese services in 1934 as an official weapon, for how else could it have been given its official title of Model 94? The Japanese semi-governmental export houses were certainly active in South America in the [1930s], but nobody there seems to have heard of this very distinctive pistol ... (Wilson n.d.: 456)

Chūō-Kōgyō "Nagoya Nambu" Type 94 pistol 23839 is dated March 1942 (Shōwa 17.3). (Amoskeag Auctions, www.amoskeagauction.com)

THE TYPE 94 REVEALED

8mm pre-1941 variant

Recoil-operated, the Type 94 pistol is locked by a separate block (**25**) that floats independently between two lugs under the chamber end of the barrel. The locking unit is controlled by cam-ways cut into the frame and locks into a transverse notch cut across the underside of the barrel housing or slide.

The barrel/slide group recoils through about 0.1in as the pistol is fired, whereafter the locking block begins its downward movement. It completely disengages after further travel through 0.1in, the barrel halting as its lug strikes the frame in front of the trigger, and the slide (**2**) runs back alone. The recoil spring (**4**) is compressed between the slide and the barrel (**3**), until it halts recoil and returns

the components to their initial position – transferring a new round from the magazine (**16**) to the chamber (**5**) and camming up the locking block into its slide recesses.

An elongated sear bar (**14**), lying in a channel on the left side of the frame, converts the vertical movement of the trigger into lateral movement of the sear through a spring-loaded intermediary plunger on top of the trigger. The cam-shaped plunger tip projects at 90 degrees to the sear bar and engages an oblique cam-way in the sear nose. The sear bar moves toward the right side of the frame as the trigger is pulled, disengaging its tail from the hammer (**11**).

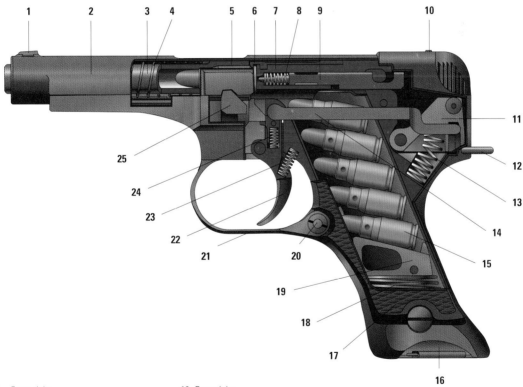

1. Front sight
2. Slide
3. Barrel
4. Recoil spring
5. Cartridge in chamber
6. Extractor
7. Bolt
8. Firing-pin spring
9. Firing pin
10. Rear sight
11. Hammer
12. Lanyard loop
13. Hammer spring
14. Sear bar
15. Cartridges in magazine
16. Magazine
17. Grip
18. Magazine spring
19. Magazine follower
20. Magazine catch nut
21. Trigger guard
22. Trigger
23. Trigger spring
24. Disconnector spring
25. Locking block

There is little doubt that the Type 94 originated as a commercial project, but also that it was not purchased by the IJA until the beginning of the Second Sino-Japanese War in July 1937. It is not entirely clear how much Nambu Kijirō contributed to its design, which differed radically from his earlier Nambu and 14th Year Type pistols.

Work was completed by 1934, if the official designation is to be believed, and the pistols were supposedly initially marketed as "Self-acting [i.e. automatic] Pistols, B-Type," though it is difficult to conclusively discredit a plausible alternative explanation that the "B-Type" (*Otsu-gata*) notation was simply a means of distinguishing between the two principal post-1937 IJA pistols – as the older 14th Year Type, on such a system, would have been the "A-Type" (*Kō-gata*).

The beginning of the Second Sino-Japanese War intensified production of 14th Year Type pistols: about 11,000 were produced by Chūō-Kōgyō in 1936, followed by 16,000 in 1937. Only about 2,300 Type 94 pistols had been produced before July 1937, however, probably on account of the Type 94's strange design, high cost compared with the cheap revolvers imported from the United States, and a genuine lack of need.

Owing to ever-growing shortages of serviceable handguns, the IJA then seized on the "Type 94"; existing stocks were purchased from Chūō-Kōgyō Kabushiki Kaisha (as Nambu-Seisakusho had become at the end of 1936) and production continued under the supervision of inspectors from Nagoya Army Arsenal. Slightly more than 71,000 pistols were produced, the observed serial-number range currently being 1–71075, before work ceased in mid-1945. The design was never revived postwar, a fate made inevitable by its odd characteristics.

Measuring 7.36in overall, with a 3.78in 8mm-caliber barrel with six-groove right-hand twist rifling, and weighing about 1lb 11oz, the Type 94 bears no resemblance whatsoever to the earlier Nambu and 14th Year Type pistols. Some features of the Type 94 resemble a Browning, although the similarity is purely superficial. Its oddly deep frame, bridged for the slide and breechblock assembly to pass through, is most distinctive. Nor can the pistol's oddly designed grip, containing the box magazine, be mistaken for anything else.

Magazine capacity was restricted to just six rounds: a retrograde step as far as combat was concerned but essential to maintain the compact dimensions demanded by aviators and tank crews. Between eight and ten rounds were considered ideal in the 1930s, but even then the 9mm FN-Browning GP Mle 35 was being offered with 13 rounds.

Some firers of the Type 94 considered the grip to be comfortable, provided the firer's hand was gloved. Wilson considered that among the Type 94's good features was the "angle of slope of the grip" (n.d.: 469B), while Moss took the view that the grip was too small and poorly shaped (1975: 75).

Type 94 pistols were manufactured exclusively by the Nambu-Seisakusho/Chūō-Kōgyō factory in Tōkyō-Kitatama, sometimes known as the Kokubunji works as its address was Hondashinden, Kokubunji-Machi, Kitatama, Tōkyō. The first examples were completed in June 1935 (Shōwa 10.6), but production was slow and fewer than 3,000 had been manufactured before the Second Sino-Japanese War commenced.

PROTOTYPES

Comparatively little is known about the development of the Nambu pistol, though there were probably several stages between concept and completion. Several large Nambu-style pistols, incorporating features of both the original A-Type ("Papa") Nambu and the 14th Year Type, survive, however. Pistol 3 is said (Leithe 1967) to have been found in Tōkyō Army Arsenal in 1946, and 15 is the highest serial number known.

Recently if somewhat tentatively identified as the "Experimental Type 'A' self-loading pistol" (*shisei kogo jidokenju*), these pistols were apparently made about 1920 under Nambu's supervision; but the design seems to have been too radical to gain acceptance, allowing some features to be incorporated in the 14th Year Type.

The prototypes' magazines hold 16 8mm cartridges, twice that of the Nambu and 14th Year Type pistols, which has led to suggestions that it was contemporaneous with the Belgian 9mm FN-Browning GP Mle 35 – the first service pistol to introduce a large-capacity, staggered-column magazine contained entirely within the butt. The origins of the GP Mle 35 date back to the 1920s, but it seems unlikely to have influenced the "Type A" if indeed the latter dates from 1920.

The action of the large pistols is essentially similar to that of the standard Nambu: operated by short recoil and locked by a propped-up block, which lies in the frame beneath the receiver and can engage a recess cut in the bolt. The pistols use the old-style hollow locking block through

Little is known about this somewhat odd-looking pistol, made in two differing patterns. Apparently recoil-operated and chambering the standard 8×22mm Nambu cartridge, it seems to date from the period in which not only what became the Type 94 pistol was developed but also the so-called Type 1 submachine gun was designed by Major-General Tokunaga Shikanosuke on the basis of Nambu Kijirō's patents. The oddly shaped butt containing a curved magazine may prove to be the link. (Author's archives)

Otherwise unmarked 8mm Experimental Type "A" prototype no. 3 shows a general affinity with the earlier "Papa," but is substantially larger and has a large-capacity magazine in its well-raked grip. (Rock Island Auction, www.rockislandauction.com)

which the receiver lug passes, with the concave face of the receiver lug providing the pivot point.

The massive frame is closed only at the rear, where the bridge forms the base for the tangent-leaf back sight. Twin coil-pattern recoil springs are used, each lying in a channel in the side of the bolt and bearing against a transverse bar through the rear of the frame. The left-side mainspring has a secondary function as the firing-pin spring, the firing-pin nose being offset toward the centerline of the bolt.

The trigger system resembles that of the 14th Year Type pistol, and the transverse magazine-release catch appears on the lower front of the butt-toe.

Despite obvious affinities with the 14th Year Type pistol, the sharply angled grip is more redolent of the German Luger or Finnish Lahti pistols. The prototype is 10.83in long, with a 6.10in barrel, and weighs about 3lb 5oz despite the lightening cuts in the receiver: bigger even than the Lahti, making the "Big Nambu" far too large no matter how good its balance might be and even though great weight combined with the low-power cartridges would make the pistol pleasant to fire.

USE
The Nambu pistols go to war

JAPANESE HANDGUNS IN SERVICE 1894–1905

One year after approval of the 26th Year Type revolver, Japan went to war with China in the First Sino-Japanese War (1894–95); less than a decade later, the IJA and the IJN confronted Tsar Nicholas II's forces in the Russo-Japanese War (1904–05).

The First Sino-Japanese War resulted from Japan's quest for supremacy in Korea, effectively China's client state but facing the Japanese islands geographically. When war was declared on August 1, 1894, most observers expected the Chinese to prevail, but the greatly outnumbered Japanese were not only prepared to fight but also better equipped. Japanese victories on land and at sea then allowed the invasion of Shandong and Manchuria; as Japanese forces had also captured the forts commanding maritime approaches to Peking (modern-day Beijing), China sought peace, with the Treaty of Shimonoseki being signed on April 17, 1895. In the long term, hostilities created a desire for reform in China that led to the 1911 Revolution and ultimately to war between China and Japan in 1937.

Like the officers of most armies, those of the IJA were expected to provide personal weapons and equipment at their own expense. Handguns could be obtained from distributors and wholesalers such as the Kawaguchiya Fire Arms Company, but also through cooperatives now generally known as "Officer's Union" but strictly named *Kaikōsha* (IJA). Based in Tōkyō with outlets generally in the paymasters' offices at divisional and regimental headquarters, *Kaikōsha* could supply officers with virtually any type of handgun – Smith & Wesson, Colt, and Harrington & Richardson revolvers, and Mauser and FN-Browning pistols among them. Long after the appearance of indigenous types of revolver and pistol, many of these imported handguns survived to serve

SWORDS AND HANDGUNS

The Japanese sword was held in reverence unparalleled in the West, and all officers were ordered to wear them after conscription was introduced in 1872. In addition, the influence of the samurai loomed large in Japanese military circles long after the Satsuma Rebellion of January–September 1877 had been crushed.

Veneration of the sword was reinforced by *bushidō* ("way of the warrior"), an ancient ethical code that placed honor above life itself. Bolstered by swordsmanship and knowledge of martial arts, and unswerving loyalty to his *daimyō* (master), a true samurai did not fear death. If threatened with loss of honor, he could regain his standing with *seppuku* ("belly cut") – a form of ritual suicide.

The strength of such feelings ensured that handguns were generally held in low esteem by IJA and IJN officers alike, especially those who came from privileged or noble backgrounds. Such innate bias unquestionably hampered the sale of Nambu pistols, and, when the time came for Japanese forces to surrender in 1945, edged weapons outnumbered handguns. Most common

were *tachi* types, with blade lengths of 25–29.5in, but there were also *wakizashi* with blade lengths of 19.5–25in and daggers known as *tanto* with guards or *aikuchi* without guards. Some were of great antiquity and outstanding examples of the swordmaker's art.

The first traditional-style sword to be mass-produced in Japan, the *kyū-guntō* ("old military style") had been introduced in 1875 and remained in production until the adoption of the Type 94 *shin-guntō* in 1934. Murata Tsuneyoshi is said to have combined a traditional Japanese double-hand *tachi*-type sword with a Western-style pommel and single-bar knucklebow. The grips were of yellow or white *samē* (sharkskin or substitute), sometimes bound with silver or gold wire, while the hilt was protected by a brass, gilded or gold-plated back-strap cast with traditional cherry blossom and chrysanthemum designs.

IJA scabbards were made of chromium-plated steel, whereas IJN patterns had bodies of *samē* and mounts of gilt or gilded steel. IJA scabbards were often protected by a leather cover and were suspended from a single ring, unlike the IJN's customary two rings.

In the Japanese military, swords remained the most prestigious weapons until the country's unconditional surrender in 1945. Here, Royal Australian Navy personnel inspect a Japanese sword and a 14th Year Type pistol typical of the large numbers that passed into Allied hands during World War II. (Australian War Memorial P00455.018, www.awm.gov.au)

An IJA first lieutenant poses at the time of the Second Sino-Japanese War with a holstered Nambu pistol and a *shin-guntō* sword based on the traditional *tachi*. Type 94 officers' swords of the pattern shown here – made principally in Toyokawa Navy Arsenal – were superseded by the Type 98, essentially similar but much easier to make. Type 95 NCOs' swords were based on the Type 94, but had machine-made fullered blades and cast-alloy or synthetic grips embossed to represent traditional binding. (Author's archives)

Japanese artillerymen debark at Chenampo, Korea, during the Russo-Japanese War. Holsters for Smith & Wesson revolvers are evident, notably behind the hilt of the sword carried by the officer standing at the right. (Author's archives)

in World War II, and to be surrendered to Allied forces at the end of hostilities. While many officers carried privately purchased Smith & Wesson revolvers, the Meiji 26th Year Type revolver of 1893 had been developed primarily as the weapon of NCOs; popularly associated with infantry service, it was also carried by cavalrymen even though swords and the Meiji 27th Year Type Murata carbine were their primary weapons.

The 26th Year Type revolver served throughout the First Sino-Japanese War and then the Russo-Japanese War, a conflict originating in claims made by both Russia and Japan to the territory not only of Manchuria but also Korea. The Russians could muster about 1.3 million men when hostilities began on February 8, 1904, but mobilization soon increased this total to 3.5 million. By comparison, the IJA had only about 325,000 men, though many were battle-hardened veterans of the First Sino-Japanese War and mobilization soon raised strength to 450,000 men.

Major engagements on land almost always ended in Japanese victory – from the battle of the Yalu River (April 30–May 1, 1904) in what is now North Korea near the border with Manchuria, to the battle of Mukden (February 20–March 10, 1905) in which 270,000 Japanese troops effectively drove 330,000 Russian soldiers out of Manchuria. Port Arthur fell to the Japanese, the Russians surrendering on January 3, 1905. Equally important was the battle of the Tsushima Straits (May 27/28, 1905), in which the Russian fleet was eviscerated by a Japanese squadron. Hostilities were formally ended on September 5, 1905, by the Treaty of Portsmouth. Victory duly boosted Japanese nationalism and the determination to exert greater influence in East Asia, while in Russia the October Revolution of 1917 can also be regarded as an indirect consequence of the Russo-Japanese War.

Particular lessons learned from fighting that ranged far and wide, often involving static warfare in trenches and strongpoints, included the need for lubricants that could protect weapons against the Siberian winter and the need for effectual machine guns. Moreover, the conflict shaped the development not only of Japanese small arms in general, but inspired the promotion of pistols in particular. There can be little doubt that the Japanese forces encountered Mauser C/96 pistols in the hands of the Russians, particularly officers who had bought them individually. Sales figures provided by Waffenfabrik Mauser show that 422 Mauser pistols had gone to Russia in 1904 followed by 1,240 in 1905, representing the largest single market outside Germany, which had taken 3,115 in the same period.

Turning to Japan's naval forces, .44 Smith & Wesson revolvers were widely distributed to Japanese marines at the time of the First Sino-Japanese War while others were held in shipboard armories for use by landing parties and prize crews. Many Smith & Wessons survived to serve during the Russo-Japanese War, even though supposedly superseded by the Meiji 26th Year Type revolver. IJN officers had to purchase their own personal-defense weapons, however, often through cooperatives known as *Suikōsha*; these were run on similar lines to the aforementioned IJA *Kaikōsha*. Consequently, a wide range of handguns were carried.

It is not clear whether Nambu pistols ever reached the front line during the Russo-Japanese War, even in small numbers. Countless swords can be linked with this period, but only the earliest "Grandpa" Nambu pistols could have made it – and then only if production and distribution was sufficiently advanced to allow it.

Japanese troops landed at Port Adam and considering attacking a Russian hospital train coming from Port Arthur are urged to exercise caution by an officer with a sword in his left hand and a holster, on his waist belt, which would most probably contain a privately purchased revolver. (Author's archives)

WORLD WAR I AND THE RUSSIAN CIVIL WAR

"Grandpa" and "Papa" Nambu pistols were likely used in Siam (known as Thailand from 1939) and China before 1914, though few details of these acquisitions have ever been found (see page 71). Others were undoubtedly sold commercially, but no official IJA adoption has yet been traced even though some examples were undoubtedly acquired by individual IJA officers – usage that was tolerated or perhaps even encouraged by the military authorities.

Virtually no evidence exists to confirm that Nambu handguns were ever used in combat during World War I. Japanese forces were involved only in a limited way, however, far from the carnage of the Western and Eastern fronts. Land operations were confined very largely to neutralizing the port of Tsingtao and the Kiautschou protectorate, ceded to Germany by China in 1898. Concluded on November 7, 1914, with the help of British forces, the successful campaign led to the Japanese capture of five German warships – the unprotected cruiser *Cormoran* and gunboats *Iltis*, *Jaguar*, *Luchs*, and *Tiger* – and possibly the impressment of 1904-pattern Parabellum ("Luger") pistols not only held in the shipboard armories but also those that had been issued to German land-based units on colonial service.

It has been claimed that some German pistols were given to Royal Navy officers involved in the seizure of the Protectorate, and that the remainder returned to Japan at the close of the campaign. At least one surviving 1904-type Parabellum bears Japanese marks on an accompanying holster, and some pistols survived to be taken as trophies by US servicemen in 1945. The quantities involved were quite small, however, as the gunboats – unlike *Cormoran*, which was issued with 28 – carried only 20 Lugers apiece and the III. Seebataillon (the marine unit serving in the Kiautschou protectorate when World War I began) is unlikely to have had more than the 77 allocated to the II. Seebataillon.

Prior to 1914, the German Empire had not only created the *Kreuzergeschwader* ("Cruiser Squadron") but was also administering

The German unprotected cruiser *Cormoran*, disarmed and then scuttled on September 28, 1914, shortly before the fall of Tsingtao, should have carried 28 1904-type Lugers and possibly an *Auslandzuschlag* ("overseas quota") of as many as 20 additional handguns. (Author's archives)

colonies in the Pacific: the Caroline, Mariana and Marshall Islands, Samoa, and Bougainville in the Solomon Islands, together with Kaiser Wilhelmsland (part of what is now New Guinea) and Herbertshöhe. By October 14, however, within a few weeks of the start of hostilities, Japanese forces occupied all one-time German possessions in the Pacific. In addition, the IJN sent the South Seas Squadron to help pursue the *Kreuzergeschwader*, and several warships – including the battlecruiser *Ibuki* and the light cruiser *Chikuma* – were detached to hunt for the raider *Emden*, then escort troop convoys and safeguard the vital sea-lanes between Europe, East Asia, and Australasia.

The Japanese also became involved in Siberia during the Russian Civil War (1917–22), owing to widespread suspicion of the anti-imperialist Bolsheviks and growing concern about the threat that could be posed to Japanese shipping by the Russian fleet based at Vladivostok. Japanese marines occupied Vladivostok from April 5, 1918, and 12,000 troops were sent to consolidate the gains; about 70,000 were ultimately deployed under Japanese control. Pro-Japanese settlements allowed commercial and industrial interests to gain a foothold until concerted attacks by Bolshevik forces, though beaten off, persuaded the authorities to announce a withdrawal on June 24, 1922, though Sakhalin remained under Japanese control until May 1925.

Service showed the "Papa" Nambu pistol to have good and bad features, which can be said of many Japanese small arms. Its better features include an excellent trigger system giving a very smooth and light pull, acceptable balance and accuracy, and the superior quality of its material and finish. On the debit side, the Japanese passion for keys, feathers, pins, and wire-springs is clearly evident, and the only "safety" device – the lever that blocks the trigger – is scarcely adequate.

Additionally, the material of the firing-pin spring rapidly weakened with age and use, until a high percentage of misfires ensued. Pockets for spare firing-pin springs were provided in the leather or canvas webbing service holsters, but the springs were rarely found in captured holsters during World War II and it can only be concluded that they had been used. Wilson believed that

The chief drawback of this pistol (apart from its light bullet) appears ... to be in the unreliability either of the striker mechanism or the ammunition. It was found on a short and rather hurried test in the field, that with one particular example ... misfires occurred in the rough proportion of 1 to 5 rounds put through the pistol; quite clearly dangerously, if not fatally, high for combat conditions. These misfired primers had in every instance been somewhat lightly struck. (Wilson n.d.: 438–39)

The potential danger that lay in the weak firing-pin spring – a misfire leaving the firer vulnerable while he cleared the weapon – negated the Nambu pistol's good balance and accuracy. It also made the pistol undesirable in combat. Most new pistols operated satisfactorily, as their firing-pin springs had not been subjected to years of progressive deterioration on tropical service; many older examples did not.

THE SECOND SINO-JAPANESE WAR

The Japanese effectively controlled Manchuria throughout the early 20th century, even though sovereignty supposedly lay with China. When the Chinese began building railways of their own to compete with the Japanese-controlled South Manchurian Railway, minor incidents became of ever-growing significance until, in September 1931, alleging that Chinese had blown up part of the track of the South Manchurian Railway near the city, the Japanese seized Mukden (modern-day Shenyang). The Japanese established the puppet state of Manchukuo in 1932 and, in the spring of 1934, declared China to be a Japanese vassal state. A minor clash between Chinese and Japanese troops at the Marco Polo Bridge, not far from Peking, on July 7, 1937, rapidly escalated into full-scale war.

RIGHT
An IJA infantry sergeant brandishes his 26th Year Type revolver at the time of the Second Sino-Japanese War. (Author's archives)

FAR RIGHT
An IJA first lieutenant wields a Mauser C/96-type pistol taken from the Chinese in Manchuria in 1937. (Author's archives)

PISTOLS FOR AVIATORS AND TANKERS

During the first part of the 20th century the Japanese military, like their contemporaries across the world, took a growing interest in aerial power and armored forces. The Imperial Japanese Naval Air Service (IJNAS) initially concentrated on the defense of the most important warships, shifting focus from battleships to aircraft carriers shortly before the Second Sino-Japanese War began. Land-based units tasked with defending the Home Islands if threatened with invasion were created in 1931, their role soon expanded to include strategic bombing. When the Second Sino-Japanese War began in July 1937, the IJNAS had 895 aircraft; by December 1941, it mustered 1,830 front-line aircraft, including 240 land-based twin-engine bombers, which were mostly of the Mitsubishi G3M type. Several of the G3M's seven-man crew were issued with handguns. While squadrons were commanded by either junior officers or senior warrant officers carrying privately purchased handguns, most pilots at this time were NCOs armed with issue handguns. The Imperial Japanese Army Air Service (IJAAS), intended to reconnoiter and provide support in cooperation with ground forces, operated 1,375 front-line aircraft in 1940. When World War II ended in August 1945, Japanese military strength estimated as totaling 6,095,000 included no fewer than 676,863 IJAAS personnel.

While accorded much less priority than aircraft production, the development and manufacture of Japanese tanks generated a similar requirement for compact self-defense weapons to be issued to NCOs and enlisted men. By the time World War II ended, Japanese tank production had included 2,300 Type 95 Ha-Gō light tanks and about 3,000 Type 97 Chi-Ha medium tanks. Though these totals compared unfavorably with the US M4 and Soviet T-34 medium tanks, production of which (all types) amounted to 49,234 and 84,070 respectively, handguns for tank crews were nevertheless required in quantity – especially in view of the almost total lack in Japanese service of weapons comparable to the British Sten Gun or the US M1 Carbine.

Japanese development and adoption of aircraft and tanks exerted a major influence on the issue of handguns by the early 1930s. Though, initially, Japanese military aviators and tank commanders were often commissioned officers, many of the crewmen were NCOs to whom sidearms were issued rather than having been purchased privately. As surviving images often suggest, however, not all aircrew or tank crewmen carried handguns in service, owing to cramped conditions and the need to wear equipment such as parachutes, life-jackets, and gas-masks. Even though space could be found inside an aircraft or a tank to stow a pistol, the Nambu and 14th Year Type pistols were much bulkier than FN-Browning pocket pistols and similar products that could be acquired commercially or through the *Kaikōsha* system. Development of a compact pistol began in the early 1930s, therefore, and it is reasonable to suppose that tests were undertaken with a variety of handguns.

As an indigenous weapon was preferable – on account of ease of production and procurement – and the fiercely nationalistic pride of the era meant that virtually any such weapon would be accepted, efficient or otherwise, development continued until prototypes were extensively tested in Manchukuo and Japan. What was to become the Type 94 pistol gained approval, allowing production to begin in June 1935 (Shōwa 10.6). Even though serial numbers had reached only 700 by the end of 1935, issues had soon been made to airmen, vehicle crews, and others who fought in extremely cramped conditions with more appropriate handguns than the bulky 14th Year Type. The Second Sino-Japanese War was the first large-scale conflict in which the Japanese forces made extensive use of the Type 94 pistol; about 2,300 had been produced when hostilities commenced in June 1937.

Owing to the unique veneration of the sword in Japanese culture, photographs of airmen and tank crewmen taken during World War II customarily focus more on edged weapons than handguns. Short-swords and daggers were often carried in aircraft or armored vehicles, not to allow crewmen to fight off their enemies after a forced landing or the abandonment of vehicles – as would be the case in Allied forces – but as a last resort. Rather than surrendering, committing suicide by *seppuku* rather than by pistol-shot was regarded as preferable.

This tank crewman, photographed in China on February 22, 1942, wears what appears to be a Nambu stud-and-slot closure holster suspended from a webbing shoulder strap on his right hip and an Arisaka rifle bayonet on the left. (Author's archives)

This 14th Year Type pistol, with the standard pre-1940 trigger guard, is pictured with a post-1940 magazine identified by the cutout or notch in the upper edge of the magazine toward the base. This was engaged by an auxiliary magazine-retaining spring added after 1940 to the front grip-strap toward the bottom of the butt. (Morphy Auctions, www.morphyauctions.com)

OPPOSITE
Two views of Nagoya-Toriimatsu 14th Year Type pistol *ro*-18175, dating from February 1944 (Shōwa 19.2), with its holster. (Rock Island Auction, www.rockislandauction.com)

Japanese forces, better prepared than the Chinese, soon seized most of the ports, many large cities east of Hankow (modern-day Hankou, part of Wuhan city), and much of the railway system. Peking and Tientsin (modern-day Tianjin) were occupied in July 1937, and the Chinese armies had been driven out of Shanghai by November. Nanking (modern-day Nanjing), the Nationalist Chinese capital, fell in December 1937, and Hankow was taken in October 1938. The Japanese then surged along the railway lines into Shansi (modern-day Shanxi) and Inner Mongolia, dominating Shantung (modern-day Shandong) and disrupting communications in the lower Yangtze valley. The IJN had command of the sea, and Japanese airmen had not only all but destroyed the Chinese Air Force but also bombed Chinese cities at will – totally oblivious to ever-rising civilian casualties. The Japanese authorities then tried to subdue Chinese resistance by blockade, and, in 1940, took advantage of the French capitulation in Europe to advance into Indochina. Yet hostilities continued far beyond Japanese expectations, often conducted by Chinese guerrilla bands. Irregular warfare of this type, in the absence of submachine guns and similarly compact weaponry with high rates of fire, placed greater dependence on the use of handguns than in more conventional campaigns. Combat was regularly undertaken at close range, where the need for rapid response favored an autoloading pistol, even though the supply of guns and ammunition could be difficult in areas where over-extended lines of communication interfered with logistics.

The challenging climate and terrain encountered by Japanese forces operating in Manchuria and China influenced Japanese handgun development. Extreme winter conditions revealed weaknesses in the

The Type 94 pistol, shown here with pistol and holster, held six rounds. It had a plain-sided, nickel-plated body and a base-plate with longitudinal lugs projecting far enough to facilitate removal from the butt. Details can vary according to the manufacturer but, during World War II, quality declined noticeably and nickel-plating gave way to bluing. The eight-round magazine of the "Grandpa" and "Papa" Nambu pistols and the seven-round magazine of the "Baby" Nambu pistol have nickel-plated sheet-metal bodies containing a follower shaped to support the cartridges and a spring to lift them into place. A separate base-block with checkered finger-grips is held in the body by two transverse pins. The wooden base of the "Grandpa" magazine was replaced by an aluminum-alloy casting on "Papa" and "Baby" pistols, but all magazines have a button attached to the right side of the follower, sliding in a slot in the body, which allows the follower to be depressed against the resistance of the spring to reload. The eight-round magazine of the 14th Year Type pistol is also broadly comparable with the Nambu types, though those manufactured after mid-1940 have a cut-out on the lower front edge of the body so that the auxiliary magazine catch fitted to the front of the pistol butt can engage satisfactorily. (Hermann Historica, www.hermann-historica.de)

14th Year Type firing pin, and also that the lack of a magazine safety was potentially problematical. Consequently, in 1932 (Shōwa 7) a magazine safety was added and revisions were made not only to the firing pin but also to its spring guide. The changes were incorporated in new production, but many of the handguns that had already reached the battlefront were recalled for modification. In addition, as a gloved finger could not easily access the trigger of the 14th Year Type pistol, the trigger guard was greatly enlarged in September 1939 (Shōwa 14.9).

About 5,850 examples of the so-called transitional model had been made by the end of 1939 (Shōwa 14), the change being implemented in the region of serial number 66750 though a degree of overlap occurred: 66753 has a new large trigger guard while 66755 retains the small pattern. In addition, many old "small guard" pistols were upgraded when returning for refurbishment.

Urban combat in China, 1939 (opposite)

Much combat in the Second Sino-Japanese War took place in towns and cities. Here, a Japanese SNLF lieutenant-commander has been hit; he has dropped the "Papa" Nambu which he has had since he joined the IJN 20 years earlier. The pistol, its holster suspended by a strap over the man's left shoulder, has landed between his legs owing to the constraint of the lanyard – running around his neck – which is attached to the loop on the rear of the pistol's frame. The Chinese infantry lieutenant carries the Mauser C/96 with which he fired the fatal shot. Popular with Chinese forces in many guises, German, Spanish, and Chinese-made variants among them, the Mauser is accompanied by a wood-bodied holster-stock hanging from a shoulder strap. In addition, he carries not only the dead officer's Type 97 *shin-gunto* but also his binoculars. Yet the lieutenant must now consider confronting the Japanese soldiers who have emerged from cover. Two men carry 38th Year Type Arisaka rifles fitted with bayonets, while the third has a pre-1940 "small guard" 14th Year Type pistol.

Photographed in Manchuria, apparently after the battles of Khalkin-Gol in 1939, these Japanese soldiers pose with a captured Soviet Degtyarev tank machine gun adapted for ground use by fitting its auxiliary bipod. The officer standing centrally wears a holstered Type 94 pistol. (Author's archives)

In January 1940 (Shōwa 15.1), an auxiliary magazine-retaining spring was added on the front of the grip. This secured the magazine in addition to the standard crossbolt. The auxiliary retainer was a good idea in view of the magazine safety, and problems arising from a lost magazine. Magazines dating later than mid-1940 have a special aperture in the front of the body to retain the cartridge follower in its lowest position; when the magazine needs replenishing, the depressor button is simply pushed down and slightly forward to lock under the notch, disconnecting the follower spring so that cartridges can be dropped into the magazine. Should the user forget to disengage the follower from its retaining notch, however, the pistol will not load because the magazine spring is not lifting the cartridge column. The auxiliary magazine-retaining spring pushes through the aperture in the front of the magazine body, reconnecting the feed system if the user has omitted to do so.

A change was made at this time to the 14th Year Type grip panels, 17 grooves replacing 25 (though nonstandard variants may be encountered). From October 1941 (Shōwa 16.10), magazines were blued instead of plated, to conserve valuable nickel for more important tasks, and internal components, previously blued, were left "in the white" to save time. In May 1942 (Shōwa 17.5), however, the use of hot-salt blue to protect components was introduced. This lasted until quality began to decline notably in the summer of 1944.

The badge visible on his right upper sleeve identifies this NCO of the Special Naval Landing Forces, though no rank insignia can be seen. He poses at the time of the Second Sino-Japanese War with a 14th Year Type pistol of the "small guard" or pre-1940 pattern, attached to the lanyard that runs over his left shoulder. A standard Arisaka rifle bayonet suspended from a shoulder strap lies on his left hip. (Author's archives)

STOCKS AND HOLSTERS

Attachment slots were milled into the grip back-strap of many "Grandpa" Nambu and TGE-made "Papa" Nambu pistols (but none of the latter manufactured in Tōkyō Army Arsenal) to accept a distinctive holster-stock customarily numbered to the individual weapon. Made in two variants, differing principally in length, the stock has a hinged lid and contains a cleaning rod and a spare magazine. A retractable tubular connector, carrying the attachment lug, protrudes from a collar forming the neck of the wooden body.

It has been suggested, on the basis of correlation between serial numbers and *chakra* (war quoit) marks, that the holster-stocks may have been introduced to accompany pistols that had gone to Thailand. This does not account for the rarity of stocks associated with the TGE-made naval pistols, however, but the idea was rapidly abandoned.

Holsters for the basic Nambu pistols – "Grandpa," "Papa," and "Baby" alike – generally took similar form. Made of good-quality cowhide, they were of so-called "clamshell" design in which the flap was molded in such a way as to keep rainwater off the pistol. Closure was effected by slipping a keyholed oval plate, riveted to the closing strap, over a stud on the lower part of the holster body. Each holster was accompanied by a cleaning rod with a slotted tip and a double-bend at the rear that ended in a screwdriver-blade to assist dismantling. The cleaning rods were initially nickel-plated, though this eventually gave way to bluing and the double-curve and peg were replaced with a simple right-angle bend.

The holster for the 26th Year Type revolver had a pouch inside the flap, closed by its own stud-and-slot, which held 18 9×22mm rimmed cartridges in individual loops. The first Nambu holsters were similar, holding 16 rounds in the pouch and a cleaning rod and a spare magazine within the body. A belt-loop and two small loops

for the shoulder-strap suspension links were sewn onto the back. The "Baby" Nambu holster was similar, but, owing to space limitations, lacked provision for the spare magazine.

The 14th Year Type holster also resembled that of the Nambu, though the pouch was altered to hold two 15-round cartridge boxes and a pocket was added to hold a spare firing pin. In addition, the pouch was closed by a strap-and-tongue system instead of stud-and-slot.

The material used was good-quality cowhide until the early part of World War II, when, sometime after the internal dimensions had been adjusted in 1940 to accept the enlarged trigger guard, shortages of leather forced the introduction of rubberized fabric. Another change concerned the closing strap, which gained a short spring-loaded connector. The keyhole-and-stud system was retained, but tension exerted by the connector when the strap was closed was intended to increase security.

The Type 94 holster, initially made of cowhide but then of pigskin and ultimately of canvas, differed from the Nambu types. A pouch stitched vertically to the front of the body contained the cleaning rod and a magazine, spare cartridges being relegated to separate pouches intended to be carried on the shoulder strap. Canvas holsters usually have an additional pouch or pocket for a spare firing pin, and, as World War II drew to a close, perhaps at the time the simplified "squareback" Type 94 appeared, simple open-mouth holsters were made in small quantities.

Officers were expected to purchase handguns commercially, so nonstandard holsters may also be found. In addition, "Papa" Nambu and 14th Year Type pistols shared similar dimensions, so their holsters were sometimes exchanged in service.

Most "Grandpa" Nambu pistols – this is 1595 – could be fitted with a distinctive holster-stock, issued with the expectation that, by fitting it to the pistol, range-of-engagement and long-range accuracy would improve. Though clearly inspired by the Mauser C/96 type, the Japanese design had a unique telescoping wrist. A lug on the stock mated with a groove cut vertically in the back-strap of the pistol grip. Many surviving "Grandpa" Nambu pistols – and, indeed, some "Papa" Nambu examples – have had these attachment grooves filled, however, and it is suspected that the authorities realized that rigid holster-stocks were of little use in the field, being awkward to carry and slow to attach. Much more common is the regulation holster, a clamshell type made of cowhide. (Rock Island Auction, www.rockislandauction.com)

Nambu and 14th Year Type pistols were accompanied by essentially similar cowhide holsters, the former with stud-and-slot closure and the latter, as shown here, usually with a spring-tensioning system to improve security. A pouch for spare cartridges lay inside the Nambu-holster flap, whereas the 14th Year Type accepted a box containing 14 rounds. A belt-loop and two suspension rings for the shoulder strap were stitched to the rear of the body. (Rock Island Auction, www.rockislandauction.com)

A comparison of two Nagoya-made pistols and their holsters: (above) 14th Year Type 17094 dated October 1943 (Shōwa 18.10) with a holster of rubberized fabric; (below) Type 94 25742, dating from May 1942 (Shōwa 17.5), with the standard cowhide holster. Note that the Type 94 holster has a pocket for a spare magazine. (Rock Island Auction, www.rockislandauction.com)

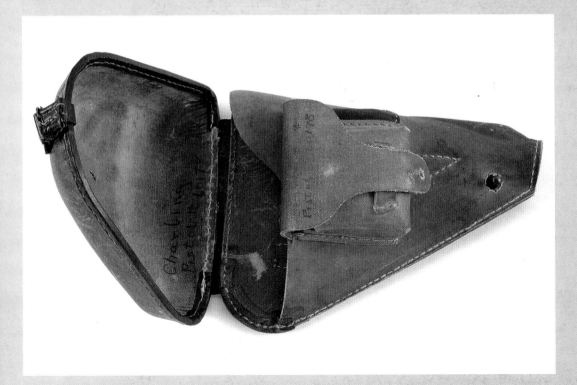

This late-war 14th Year Type holster, accompanying Nagoya-Toriimatsu pistol *i*-60178 dating from December 1942, was captured by US Army Lieutenant Henry Larson Charling in 1944. Note how the ammunition pouch, with a separate flap retained by a strap-and-loop, is stitched to the front of the body. (Morphy Auctions, www.morphyauctions.com)

PEARL HARBOR AND AFTER

The attack on Pearl Harbor on December 7, 1941, plunged Japan into conflict with the United States, the British Empire, and their allies, pitching Japanese forces into combat across the Pacific and South East Asia. After Japanese forces rapidly seized Hong Kong, Singapore, Burma, the Dutch East Indies, the Philippines, and many Pacific islands, the Allied forces halted and then started to reverse the Japanese expansion. US and Allied forces steadily retook islands such as Guam and Iwo Jima, often at terrible cost in lives, until the Japanese Home Islands were threatened.

As their situation deteriorated, Japanese forces ran increasingly short of equipment. This was partly due to the inability of the manufacturers – military and civilian alike – to produce weapons quickly enough to replace those that had been lost. The problem had been evident earlier when the Japanese armed forces were substantially enlarged as the theaters of conflict expanded and casualty rates climbed alarmingly. At the beginning of the Second Sino-Japanese War in July 1937, the IJA fielded about 600,000 men, the total rising to 1,015,000 by 1939; some 3,000,000 are reported to have been engaged in China alone by 1945. As in other countries' armed forces, this massive expansion of Japanese military manpower entailed the readoption and/ or modernization of older weapons, the streamlining of weapon manufacturing processes, and the seizure and use of captured weapon types.

During the conflict, many original Nambu pistols – mainly "Papa" but occasionally "Grandpa" types – were used, generally by higher ranking officers who had purchased them earlier and had retained them after the introduction of the much more commonly encountered 14th Year Type pistol, an aesthetically less attractive product characterized by its inferior finish.

One of this group holds a Type 94 pistol. Headbands, often adorned with emblems and slogans, were widely worn by Japanese aircrew to promote their missions. Featuring an open fan between *kanji* characters reading "Protect Nation," one such item was presented by the commander of the army flight group in the Philippines before the *Tokubetsu kokkahogo kōgeki butai* ("Special National Protection Attack Force") took part in the battle for Leyte in December 1944. (Author's archives)

In addition, service-pattern handguns were carried aboard the countless ships used during the attacks on Pacific Islands. Typical of these vessels was the coastal freighter *Shosei Maru*, requisitioned by the IJN in October 1938 to serve as an auxiliary gunboat until rerated in February 1942 as a transport. Ultimately sunk in 1944, *Shosei Maru* was allocated – in addition to two 12cm guns – two Type 92 machine guns and one 11th Year Type light machine gun, together with an unspecified number of Type 38 Arisaka rifles and 14th Year Type pistols.

Consequently, many Nambu pistols were retrieved by Allied forces once the Pacific Islands had been recaptured. For example, the Australian War Memorial collection includes Nagoya-made 14th Year Type pistol 47506, dating from April 1938 (Shōwa 13.4); associated with the 1st Sasebo SNLF, it was found in Rabaul on New Britain by an Australian military-history field team after hostilities had ceased.

As far as production of the 14th Year Type was concerned, Chūō-Kōgyō reached pistol 99999 in October 1941. The serial numbers then recommenced at *i*-1 and production was resumed. Pistol *i*-8948 was manufactured in August 1942, but production was comparatively slow.

Work continued until the late summer of 1944, when priority may have been given to the Type 99 light machine gun and the Type 94 pistol, which was easier to manufacture than the 14th Year Type.

US Ordnance Department estimates taken from Japanese records are said to suggest an output of 16,138 14th Year Type pistols in 1939, 15,002 in 1940, and 16,773 in 1941, slowing perceptibly to 8,156 in 1942, 7,156 in 1943, and a mere 1,953 in 1944. Pistol *i*-20292, dating from August 1944 (Shōwa 19.8), is currently the highest-known number. No Chūō-Kōgyō 14th Year Type pistols are known to have been manufactured in 1945, though some Nagoya-Toriimatsu pistols may have incorporated Chūō-Kōgyō components.

Manufacture of 14th Year Type pistols began in the Chigusa factory of Nagoya Army Arsenal in late 1926, but had stopped in late 1932. Nagoya Army Arsenal had inspected and accepted pistols manufactured by Nambu-Seisakusho/Chūō-Kōgyō, however, and the Toriimatsu factory resumed production of the 14th Year Type in December 1941. The first pistols, assumed to have come from a preproduction run intended to perfect manufacturing techniques, bore an additional "00" mark above the first two digits of serial numbers observed to run from 50001 to 50185. It has been suggested that "00" denoted nonstandard pistols, often embodying minor changes, which were not to be issued for service, but a reversion to conventional numbering had been made by February 1942 (Shōwa 17.2).

Work continued rapidly, an "*i*" prefix distinguishing the first series of Toriimatsu-made pistols, ending in November 1943 (Shōwa 18.11) to be replaced by "*ro*," denoting the second series numbered from 1 to at least 73291 dating from August 1945 (Shōwa 20.8).

While 14th Year Type pistols completed before the middle of 1940 were manufactured from good materials and displayed acceptable surface

finish, the grade of the materials and the quality of finish declined steadily until, by the beginning of 1943, the products had become noticeably inferior. By 1944 the quality had declined even further — and the last few pistols manufactured in 1945 were among the worst service handguns ever made. Their components fitted extraordinarily badly and their surface finish consisted of little more than tool marks and blemishes. As Leithe notes (1967), quantity was prioritized over quality.

The US Army estimated that the Nagoya-Toriimatsu facilities were capable of producing 20,000 Type 94 and 45,000 14th Year Type pistols per annum in 1944–45, though these targets were never reached. Output was undoubtedly restricted, however, once the factory had been badly damaged by periodic Allied air raids toward the end of hostilities.

Shown with the rarely encountered canvas holster – which tended to deteriorate rapidly in the tropics – late-war "squareback" Type 94 pistol 69185 dated March 1945 (Shōwa 20.3), was retrieved from Okinawa by US Army Sergeant Earl Kenneth May of Milford, Indiana, at the end of World War II. It had been taken from a Japanese soldier who had committed suicide to avoid the ignominy of capture. (Pre98 Antiques, www.pre98.com)

Tankers in the Pacific, 1944 (overleaf)

Somewhere in the Pacific, a Japanese Type 95 light tank, designed for reconnaissance and lightly armored, has shed its track owing to a broken link. Two of its crew discuss the situation. The lieutenant, leaning on the front mudguard, carries a Type 94 pistol, while his driver, ranking as sergeant, carries a Meiji 26th Year Type revolver in a holster on his right hip, with the lanyard worn diagonally round the torso. Meanwhile, an apprehensive infantry private armed with a 38th Year Type Arisaka rifle awaits orders from a captain holding a post-1940 14th Year Type pistol with the enlarged trigger guard. The holster-strap runs over his left shoulder, with a map-case strap on the right. The captain has just seen great danger – a Lockheed P-38 Lightning, known as "the Whispering Assassin," is about to attack.

"Squareback" Type 94 pistol 70768, dating from June 1945 (Shōwa 20.6), clearly shows the declining production standards and a greatly simplified open-mouth holster. (Heritage Auctions, www.heritageauction.com)

The design of the firing pin was changed with effect from June 1942, Shōwa 17.6, but seems to have been planned sometime previously in response to complaints from the battlefield. The firing pin, originally 2.87in long with a 1.85in guide, was replaced with a 2.56in firing pin and 2.13in guide, the diameter of the firing-pin tip being enlarged and the clearance hole in the bolt being changed to allow the strengthened tip to reach the primer of the chambered cartridge.

Other changes made to the 14th Year Type pistol to simplify and therefore accelerate production included the use of round-headed trigger pins, introduced in February 1942 (Shōwa 17.2) and used on about 12,000 pistols made until replaced in January 1943 (Shōwa 18.1) by the flush-milled pins in countersunk holes that distinguished 88,000 pistols made prior to November 1943 (Shōwa 18.11).

Third-variation guns, about 8,300 being made from Shōwa 18.11 onward, were basically second-type guns with *ro*-prefix numbers, while the fourth type had minor changes in the sights and substituted a finely knurled cocking knob for the flanged type in December 1943 (Shōwa 18.12). This version was in full production by January 1944 (Shōwa 19.1), 6,700 being made, but noticeably coarser knurling and alterations to the grips appeared in February 1944 on the first of about 48,000 14th Year Type fifth-variation pistols numbered from *ro*-18000. Grooves cut laterally into the wood grips of Toriimatsu-made pistols, however, which had settled to 24 per side after occasional irregularities, were abandoned in November 1944 (Shōwa 19.11) to produce the so-called "slab grip" fifth-production variant; about 8,800 had been completed by June 1945 (Shōwa 20.6).

THE NORTH CHINA 19TH YEAR TYPE PISTOL

As World War II ran its course, and the Japanese situation began to deteriorate as the Allies threw ever-growing forces into the Asia–Pacific theater of operations, serious shortages of weapons became apparent. War with China had been underway since July 1937, and the formation of the Greater East Asia Ministry (大東亜省, *Daitōashō*) in September 1942 was intended to exploit manufacturing resources in Manchuria and South East Asia. Consequently, standard Arisaka rifles were manufactured by four metalworking businesses in Tientsin (modern-day Tianjin) and a variety of small arms were manufactured in quantity in Mukden (modern-day Shenyang).

No production of standard handguns, 14th Year Type and Type 94 pistols, was undertaken – but a near-copy of the former was produced in small numbers. Identified on the left side of the frame as "North China 19 Type" (北支一九式拳銃, *kitashi ichikyu shiki kenju*), its intention was to ensure that Japan's China Expeditionary Army was not unduly affected by disruption of supplies owing to the steadily rising losses of Japanese shipping in the China Sea. It is believed that the North China Engineering Company, based in Peking (modern-day Beijing), was the actual manufacturer while inspection and acceptance was undertaken in Tientsin Arsenal. US Army sources suggest that 2,000 pistols were ordered, but production was minuscule.

The Type 19 pistol, despite its external similarity with the 14th Year Type pistol, incorporates several important changes that effectively simplified manufacture. It is not clear whether this was done simply to suit the facilities of the North China Engineering Company or as a result of efforts to address complaints from combat. Though the Type 19 shares the magazine of the 14th Year Type, the latter's auxiliary magazine spring set into the front grip-strap of the service pattern was abandoned. The frame and trigger guard were forged as a single part, thus avoiding the two-part 14th Year Type construction and eliminating the magazine safety, but increasing weight to about 2lb 8oz.

A radial lever was added at the right-side front of the frame to facilitate dismantling; the barrel was simply pressed against a hard surface once the magazine and cocking knob had been removed, then the dismantling catch was rotated downward to allow the barrel unit to be pulled forward and off the frame.

The Type 19 safety catch lies on the left-side rear of the frame, behind the grip, where it could be applied by the firing hand. It locks only the sear — not also the action as in the 14th Year Type pistol — but is much more effectual.

The Type 19 pistol's wood grips have 19 horizontal grooves instead of 24. The pistols were originally blued, with some case-hardened components. The pistols required considerable hand finishing and it is suspected that their components were not truly interchangeable, as individual components will often display an assembly number that differs from the serial number.

World War II ended before mass-production of the Type 19 pistol had got underway, the highest known serial number being 55. The North China Engineering Company factory was taken over on behalf of the Chinese People's Liberation Army (PLA), however, and – at least for a short period – manufacturing began again. Chinese-made pistols, numbered in a new series from 001 to at least 093, show a few minor changes. These are confined largely to markings, particularly related to the safety catch, but a one-piece dismantling catch was fitted, the sear was simplified, the diameter of the cocking knob was somewhat reduced, and what had been machine-grooved grips gave way to hand-cut grooves that can vary in number. The concentric-circle Tientsin Arsenal mark was replaced by the ideograph *ni* ("two"), which could suggest that the authorities acknowledged the new pistols to be "second pattern." Once again, output was small.

Type 19 pistol 076. Though broadly comparable with the 14th Year Type pistol, differences are obvious in the design of the safety lever and the addition of a dismantling catch. (Rock Island Auction, www.rockislandauction.com)

This 14th Year Type pistol, 39111 of the pre-1940 "small guard" type, was manufactured by Chūō-Kōgyō and is dated November 1937 (Shōwa 12.11). It was acquired at World War II's end by Staff Sergeant Adam Albert Kirchofer of the 35th Infantry Regiment, US Army. (Rock Island Auction, www.rockislandauction.com)

The Toriimatsu factory continued to manufacture the pistols until the summer of 1945, US Ordnance Department records suggesting that 1,329 14th Year Type pistols were accepted in May, 655 in June, 1,083 in July, and apparently none in August though modern-day analysis suggests that as many as 500 pistols may have borne August dates. 14th Year Type pistols *ro*-72027 and *ro*-72028 were found unfinished in Toriimatsu after Japan had capitulated in August 1945. They have three-flange retraction grips rather than the plain-knurled or plain-surface variety, but the factory may simply have been using old components.

A comparatively small number of what are now termed "very last ditch" 14th Year Type pistols were manufactured as World War II drew to a close. The manufacturing facilities had been badly damaged by Allied air raids, and so the pistols, sometimes numbered in the 73344–76464 group, often had mismatched Nagoya and Chūō-Kōgyō components. Some frames were left "in the white," while magazine-retaining springs, lanyard loops, and magazine-safety blocks were omitted in what proved to be a vain hope of accelerating production.

Type 94 pistol production never attained spectacular heights, as only a little over 71,000 were manufactured in the ten years beginning in June 1935 and ending – as far as serial numbers can testify – in the summer of 1945. Output rose from 6,813 in 1941 (beginning in the region of pistol 15546) to 19,916 in 1944 (observed serial numbers 46164–66250), but then went into decline.

In addition to pistols made in Toriimatsu, components including ready-numbered frames in the 26000–29000 group were sent in 1942 to a subsidiary factory in Niikura, which was apparently lying idle. About 2500 Type 94 pistols were subsequently returned to Nagoya for inspection, those that were accepted being "off date" as their marks read Shōwa 18.6 to 18.8 (June–August 1943) instead of "17.6" (June 1942) found on Toriimatsu-assembled pistols from the same group.

Occasional machining changes had been incorporated, such as variations in the vertical aperture in the Type 94 slide rib, while the trigger and hammer pivots changed from split pins to rounded slot-head screws, and then to flush-fitted slot-head screws from November 1937 (Shōwa 12.11) onward. Other changes included flush-machining what had been a raised step at the rear of the sear bar and altering the adjoining frame contours appropriately, while the bolt was somewhat simplified in February 1939 (Shōwa 14.2).

Poor finish and surprisingly rough machining could be seen even on pistols dating from 1941 (Shōwa 16), and by December 1942 (Shōwa 17.12) not only were tool marks becoming increasingly obvious but also only visible surfaces were being polished. By April 1943 (Shōwa 18.4), surfaces had become very rough and components-fit could be sloppy. By December 1944 (Shōwa 19.12), blued finish was very thin and plain wooden grips had been introduced.

As the accompanying papers dating from December 1945 testify, Type 94 pistol 21649, manufactured by Chūō-Kōgyō in November 1943 (Shōwa 18.11), returned to the United States with Technician Third Grade William Joseph Gleich. (Amoskeag Auctions, www.amoskeagauction.com)

Then came the introduction of the so-called "squareback" slide, pistol 66386, currently the earliest known example, dating from January 1945 (Shōwa 20.1). Back sights were simplified and extractors were crudely fitted: the quality of the very last Type 94 pistols was terrible, lacking components such as lanyard loops and cover plates fitted to the frames. In addition, few of them bear any markings.

It is assumed that the Nambu/Chūō-Kōgyō/Nagoya-Toriimatsu conglomerate accorded 14th Year Type pistols priority, presumably as they were infantry weapons; issue of the Type 94 pistol was generally restricted to aircrew, tank crews, and some officers, and so relatively smaller quantities were required. It is also possible that an ever-increasing amount of hand finishing acted as a brake, but it is also clear that production did not show an especially marked increase toward the end of World War II.

As World War II ran its course, Japanese troops often fought to the death rather than surrender, for fear of disgracing the emperor, and losses mounted steeply. Suicide by ritual *seppuku* ("belly cut") was considered most acceptable, but was often undertaken with the aid of a Nambu pistol when time was short. In this way, on August 24, 1945, General Tanaka Shizuichi, one-time head of the War College and commander of the

1st Imperial Guards Division, shot himself in the heart to avoid the ignominy of acknowledging the arrival of US occupation forces in Japan. In another grim example, early in the morning of August 30, 1945, the IJN's Captain Ariizumi Tatsunosuke shot himself through the mouth after his submarine *I-401* had been surrendered to the US Navy.

Harry Derby (1981: 109–10) highlights the story of 14th Year Type pistol 557, manufactured in Nagoya in July 1928 (Shōwa 3.7), which Major Itō Toyotomi was carrying while serving Major-General Nishida Yoshimi as headquarters staff officer. When US forces launched Operation *Catchpole* to capture Eniewetok Atoll, Engebi, and Parry islands on February 18, 1944, Itō was sheltering in the Parry Island command bunker, where he fell victim to an order from landing-force commander Brigadier General Thomas Eugene Watson "to wipe out all remaining 'underground' Japanese troops" (Derby 1981: 110). American units often followed instructions to ensure that none of their opponents survived, while at the same time retrieving many weapons. Even more were handed over when the fighting ended, as documents and photographs eloquently testify.

Japanese soldiers surrender their weapons, including a Smith & Wesson revolver and a "large guard" 14th Year Type pistol on the table. (US National Archives)

On September 10, 1945, the commander of the Japanese 37th Army in Borneo, Lieutenant-General Baba Masao – executed on August 7, 1947, as a war criminal – surrendered a Nambu pistol and a sword to Major General George Frederick Wootten, commanding 9th Australian Division. Typical of large-scale handovers, in September 1945 Japanese troops surrendered 87 handguns to 20th Australian Infantry Brigade, commanded by Brigadier Victor Windeyer. Wilson recorded the 76 Japanese-made pistols as including five Nambus, 54 14th Year Type, and 17 Type 94, together with four .32 Colt Pocket Models, three "Browning New Model .32," a 1907-type .32 Savage, a 9mm KNIL Vickers-Parabellum, and two .38 Smith & Wesson revolvers.

In addition, many servicemen – US forces in particular – took Nambu pistols home as souvenirs, many accompanied by release papers signed by the men's superiors. Consequently, the Nambu pistol assumed a far greater significance in the postwar US commercial market than any Japanese handgun had previously achieved.

IMPACT
The Nambu in context

Though the Nambu pistol and its derivatives were preeminent as far as Japanese forces were concerned, production was surprisingly small by Western standards. It has been estimated that output of the 14th Year Type pistol totaled about 282,300, the largest contributor being the Toriimatsu factory operated by Nagoya Army Arsenal (perhaps 126,500 from December 1941 until August 1945), and that about 71,250 Type 94 pistols were produced. While these figures derive principally from serial-number analysis, and do not necessarily account for pistols that had been rejected at the proof or inspection stages, they are to a large extent supported by surviving records seized by US Army investigators after 1945.

Such quantities fell far short of the output of Japan's rivals, however. For example, Mauser-Werke is said to have made 246,685 P 38s in the fiscal years running from October 1, 1942, to September 30, 1944; Remington-Rand contributed 958,764 M1911A1 Colt-Brownings to the inventory in 1943–45; and the Soviet Union produced 282,388 Tokarev pistols in 1941–42 despite the dislocation of production caused by the German invasion of the Soviet Union in the summer of 1941.

CAPTURED PISTOLS IN JAPANESE SERVICE

Taking weaponry from the enemy was an obvious way of answering manufacturing shortfall. Supplementing matériel that had been captured in China once war began in the summer of 1937, therefore, British and Australian equipment came not only from the capture of Singapore and Malaya in 1941 but also from the Japanese surge westward into Burma and southward into New Guinea; US weaponry was retrieved in quantity

This 1906-type KNIL Luger, manufactured by Vickers and fitted with a barrel dating from 1928, was retrieved on December 24, 1945, by an Australian Military History field team from No. 4 Repair & Salvage Depot on Labuan Island. It had seen service with Japanese forces fighting locally. (Australian War Memorial RELAWM20334.001, www.awm.gov.au)

from the Philippines; and the Dutch East Indies provided large numbers of firearms that had been used by regular troops stationed in colonies and by the Koninklijk Nederlands Indisch Leger (Royal Netherlands East Indies Army).

Among the impressments were Chinese C/96 Mausers (supplied from Germany, Spanish-made clones, or manufactured locally), British Webley and Enfield revolvers, and US M1911A1 Colt-Browning pistols. Limited numbers of Nagant "gas-seal" revolvers and Tokarev pistols were taken from Soviet forces in China and Manchuria, and sizable quantities of Dutch revolvers and Lugers in the East Indies. The KNIL had adopted a 9mm 1906 or "New Model" Luger in April 1910, as the M1911, to replace the obsolescent M1891 Hembrug revolver: 4,181 pistols had been supplied by Deutsche Waffen- und Munitionsfabriken in 1911–13, followed by 6,000 ordered from Vickers in 1919, and 3,820 had come from Berlin-Karlsruher Industrie Werke in 1928.

There was also a wide range of handguns that had been purchased individually, usually by officers, or taken from the indigenous populations of territory overrun by the Japanese forces.

LAST-DITCH PISTOLS

The most radical of the Japanese attempts to make last-ditch firearms concerns what are now generally known to collectors as *hinawa-ju* ("fire-rope guns"), but were customarily designated "national simplified pistols" (国民簡易拳銃, *kokumin kani kenjū*, or 全国簡易拳銃, *zenkoku kani kenjū*). These primitive *tanegashima*-like single-shot matchlocks were intended to arm millions of personnel who were to provide home-defense if Allied forces were to set foot on the Japanese Home Islands.

Excepting the most basic characteristics, each *hinawa-ju* was one of a kind, made by workshops with only the most basic machine-tools, or by individuals who possessed at least some gunmaking abilities. The occasional example exhibits unusual features, such as rotating collars to keep water out of the touch-hole or appearance based broadly on the 14th Year Type. Whether the matchlocks would have survived firing their first shot can be debated in many cases, but, fortunately, none were ever fired in anger. Practically none survive.

OTHER JAPANESE-MADE PISTOLS

Chambered for the 7.65mm Auto (.32 ACP) cartridge and measuring just 4.49in long with a 2.83in barrel, the blowback pistol known as the **Inagaki** (稲垣式, *Inagaki shiki*) has a distinctive "IS" monogram on the right-side rear of the frame. The designer, Inagaki Iwakichi, was born *c*.1872; he served as an engineer at Tōkyō Artillery Arsenal during the time of Nambu Kijirō's superintendency. Resigning his post in 1924, after the devastating Great Kantō earthquake of September 1, 1923, Inagaki founded a sporting-gun workshop in Tōkyō's Suginami district. Among his designs was the pistol protected by Japanese patent 144612, a 7.65mm example being offered in 1941 to the First Army Technical Institute for testing.

Inagaki duly obtained permission to begin production of the pistol. No officially sanctioned approval has been authenticated, but several pistols are known with anchor marks and it has been speculated that they had been purchased by the IJN specifically for issue to aircrew. It seems unlikely that more than 500 were manufactured, however; the highest recorded serial number is 391. Quality is good, reflecting manufacture in the early stages of World War II; there are two recoil springs, and the safety lever – oddly marked "F" and "S" – lies on the left-side rear of the frame beneath the slide-retraction grooves. The detachable magazine held eight rounds.

In 1941, Inagaki altered the basic design to chamber the 8×22mm Nambu cartridge, submitting a prototype to the ordnance authorities. Larger and heavier than the 7.65mm version, the 8mm pistol was marked *Inagaki shiki* on the right side of the frame above the grip, ejected upward instead of to the right, and the safety lever was replaced by a vertically sliding button. Tested in 1942, problems with the recoil springs caused the Inagaki pistol to be rejected: no improvements seem to have been made and the design passed into history.

Designed by gunsmith Hamada Bunji and manufactured in Tōkyō by Nippon Jyuki Kabushiki Kaisha (Japan Gun Co. Ltd), the **Hamada** (浜出式, *Hamada shiki*) was another Japanese attempt to answer the terrible shortfall in handgun supplies as US and Allied forces threatened Japanese dominance. Though features such as barrel attachment, dismantling process, and firing-pin design had been protected by patents granted to Hamada in 1943, the pistol itself was adapted from the 1910-type FN-Browning that had proved popular with Japanese officers who purchased their personal weapons through commercial channels.

The first Hamada pistol, chambering the 7.65mm Auto (.32 ACP) cartridge and fitted with a nine-round magazine, was submitted for official trial in 1941. Production began soon afterward, and as many as 4,500 pistols, in several recognizably different subvariants, may have been manufactured in Tōkyō until the spring of 1944. Most of the pistols are said to have been sent to China, however, which may explain why very few survive and information is so difficult to obtain. Military trials were not as encouraging as Hamada had hoped, but the IJA showed interest in what was seen as an easily made alternative to the Type 94 pistol. Hamada submitted an 8mm pistol to the First Army Technical Institute in 1942, but several features were criticized and the institute's Major Yato Kenji became involved in development.

What has sometimes been identified as the *Hake-shiki* is said to have been approved in June 1943 (Shōwa 18.6). Small quantities were then produced in a converted textile factory in Notobe, 500 being inspected in Nagoya Army Arsenal from February 1944 (Shōwa 19.2) onward. These are said to have been followed by 1,000 in 1945, and several thousand sets of unassembled components were allegedly found by the US authorities after the war's end. Examples of the 8mm Hamada *Ni-shiki* (Type 2) pistol are very rarely encountered, however. Lacking the hold-open system of the 7.65mm version but fitted with a magazine safety, the Type 2 was 6.93in long, weighed about 1lb 12oz, and had a six-round magazine.

Made in China toward the end of World War II but looking very much like a copy of the 1903-type FN-Browning, the **Sugiura** (杉浦式, *Sugiura shiki*) was chambered for either 6.35mm or 7.65mm Browning (.25 and .32 ACP) ammunition, popular rounds used with the European and US-made pistols that had been bought in quantity by individual Japanese officers in peacetime.

Assumed to have been supplied to the IJA's China Expeditionary Force, the eight-shot 6.35mm pistol was about 5.51in long and weighed about 1lb; the 7.65mm version, also with an eight-cartridge magazine, was 7.09in long and weighed about 2lb. Comparatively well made, Sugiura pistols nevertheless show signs of hand finishing. Precisely how many were produced before

This 7.65mm Hamada pistol is dated January 1933 (Shōwa 1.8). (Rock Island Auction, www.rockislandauction.com)

This 7.65mm Inagaki pistol is numbered 160. (Rock Island Auction, www.rockislandauction.com)

The slide marking on 8mm Hamada pistol 41, sometimes misinterpreted as "12 Shiki," actually features the star-like identifier of the Notobe factory and "2 Shiki." (Rock Island Auction, www.rockislandauction.com)

hostilities ended is not known. Serial numbers of pistols manufactured under Japanese supervision run to at least 224 (6.35mm) and 3323 (7.65mm), though there is a suspicion that numbers of the 7.65mm pistols may have begun at 1001 as none have been recorded below 1012.

Once again, however, work continued under the aegis of the Chinese PLA. A serrated safety-lever head replaced the former round button style, though this change had already been made on later-production Japanese wartime products. The grip panels of Chinese-made pistols are more finely checkered, and there are usually (but not invariably) 15 slide-retraction grooves instead of 16.

Chinese serial numbers may have continued the Japanese range, the lowest recorded being 3343, and run up to at least 5839. Most slides display what has been identified as a "North China Industry" mark prefixed by a five-point star.

Two views of 7.65mm Sugiura pistol 1850, with a close-up of markings found on the slide and frame of pistol 1832. (Rock Island Auction, www.rockislandauction.com)

JAPANESE HANDGUNS IN CONTEXT

The 14th Year Type pistol, the principal Japanese infantry handgun, was just one of many pistols to see service in the Pacific during World War II. Among its rivals were the US M1911A1 Colt-Browning, the Soviet Tokarev, and a variety of Chinese Mauser C/96 pistols that included Spanish- and Chinese-made copies. British and associated forces had Webley and Enfield revolvers, not so very far removed from the surviving Meiji 26th Year Type revolvers that were occasionally pressed into service in the Pacific.

The autoloaders, though differing in detail, followed the same general pattern. They all had single-action lockwork – an area in which double-action revolvers had an advantage in combat – and were recoil-operated. Overall length and weight were generally comparable, magazine capacity ranging from seven for the Colt-Browning to ten for the Mauser C/96.

Handling qualities varied, however. The Mauser balances a little oddly, owing to the mass of the magazine ahead of the trigger and the small butt. In addition, the butts of the Colt-Browning and the Tokarev are much squarer to the bore-axis than the well-raked butts of the Nambu and 14th Year Type pistols. In snap-shooting, therefore, the "pointability" of the Japanese pistols is advantageous, as the target is acquired almost instinctively.

Variation can also be seen in "stopping power," as the 8×22mm Nambu cartridge was considerably weaker than the 7.62×25mm Tokarev, 7.63×25mm Mauser, 9×19mm Parabellum, and .45 ACP M1911 types. Though such discrepancies counted for little in close-quarter combat through the jungles and beaches of the Pacific theater of operations, they did have an effect firstly on training and then in service. Though much has been written about the importance of "stopping power," the muzzle energy of bullets such as the .45 M1911 (.45 ACP) is quite useless if the firer cannot hit the target because of excessive recoil or flinch. It can surely be argued that the chances of getting the first round on target, and then firing a second if need be, are more important than excessive theoretical considerations of energy and stopping power.

The 14th Year Type pistol is widely regarded as more accurate than many of its rivals. This was partly due to lack of recoil arising from the use of comparatively low-powered ammunition, which allowed sights to be realigned on a target for a second shot far more easily than with the powerful .45 Colt-Browning.

The small physique of the average Japanese soldier had been an important factor in the choice of the original 8×22mm Nambu cartridge, as it had been on the introduction of a relatively low-powered 6.5mm rifle pattern a decade or so earlier. The Japanese disliked the recoil of even the ex-KNIL 9mm Parabellums captured in the Netherlands East Indies during World War II. They would not have been keen to fire the .45 M1911A1 Colt-Browning, for which Wilson had a considerable liking and was apt to use as his yardstick. This became clear in the postwar years, when standard US Army weapons replaced the Japanese pistols in military and law-enforcement service.

The most damning verdict on the 14th Year Type pistol is Wilson's, but he had at least taken the opportunity to assess the value of the

Japanese weapon under combat conditions – not in a safe area, or a base camp located well behind the lines. Even allowing for his notoriously low opinion of anything that was Japanese, his assessment is quite accurate; for example, the 14th Year Type's magazine "safety," the poor quality of the firing-pin spring and the method of magazine removal are bad features, fully deserving criticism. He stated that: "the Year 14 pistol was a thoroughly bad weapon without redeeming features of any sort, in fact the most stupid modern pistol yet encountered. Its quite astonishingly bad combination of poor design, soft material, bad workmanship, negligible stopping power and general difficulty in management are quite unique ..." (Wilson n.d.: 455). In addition, the 14th Year Type pistol does have noteworthy features, though in practice they scarcely offset its many serious deficiencies. They included a light and pleasant trigger pull, acceptable combat sights, reasonable accuracy, and – above all – light recoil.

The principal handguns used in the Pacific campaign are shown here to scale. Top to bottom: the US .45 M1911A1 Colt-Browning, the Japanese 8mm 14th Year Type, the British .38in No. 2 Mk 1* Enfield revolver, the Japanese 9mm Meiji 26th Year Type revolver, a German-made 7.63mm Mauser C/96 with Chinese marks, the Japanese 8mm Type 94, and the Soviet 7.62mm Tokarev. (Morphy Auctions, www.morphyauctions.com)

AMMUNITION AND PERFORMANCE

The perfected 8×22mm Nambu cartridge adopted in January 1929 (Shōwa 4.1) had a jacketed lead-alloy cored bullet, 0.320in in diameter and weighing 102 grains, held within a bottlenecked brass case measuring 0.844in overall; cartridge length was 1.243in. The bullets of ball rounds were cupro-nickel or tin jacketed, until restricted to copper from 1942 onward. The charge of 4.6 grains of smokeless propellant gave a muzzle velocity of about 1,030ft/sec in the 14th Year Type pistol, yielding energy amounting to 242ft-lb – appreciably less than the 7.62×25mm Tokarev, 7.63mm Mauser, 9mm Parabellum, and .45 ACP cartridges.

Cartridges were packaged in 50-round boxes until the introduction of the 14th Year type pistol, when 14-round boxes were substituted to fit the ammunition pouch inside the holster.

In addition to ball rounds, dummies were made in 7mm and 8mm. Intended for instructional and drill purposes, these usually have a knurled ring around the lower part of the body.

Use of the 8×22mm Nambu cartridge was restricted to the Nambu, 14th Year Type, and Type 94 pistols and the Type 100 submachine gun. Production of the Type 100 in Nagoya Army

A typical 8×22mm Nambu bottlenecked cartridge, loaded with a cupro-nickel jacketed bullet. (Author's archives)

Arsenal probably did not exceed 8,500, however, leaving the Japanese woefully short of light automatic weapons. By way of comparison, 606,694 M3 "Grease Guns" were manufactured for US forces and even this total pales by comparison with the manufacture prior to August 1945 of 404,383 9mm Mk II Sten Guns by BSA Guns Ltd, 876,886 Mk III Sten Guns by Lines Brothers Ltd, and no fewer than 1,983,111 Mk II and Mk IIS Sten Guns by the Royal Ordnance Factory in Fazakerley.

The 7×20mm Nambu cartridge confined to the "Baby" Nambu was essentially a smaller version of the 8×22mm Nambu pattern. The bottleneck case, about 0.780in long, contributed to an overall cartridge length of 1.055in. The jacketed lead-core bullet, 0.279in in diameter, weighs a mere 56 grains but attains a muzzle velocity of about 790ft/sec; consequently, its muzzle energy, 80ft-lb, is appreciably greater than the notoriously ineffective – but very popular – 6.35mm Auto (.25 ACP), so it could easily inflict a fatal wound at close range.

Performance of the cartridge could be unpredictable, due in part to the excessively damp conditions in which ammunition was often stored, but also to the notoriously weak firing-pin spring of the 14th Year Type pistol. Wilson, stationed in Borneo, seized his opportunity to test the certainty of action in pistols surrendered after September 1945. He reported that

> ... these pistols [three 14th Year Types and two Type A Nambus] were in poor condition; they were battered, rusty and had presumably seen much service. Ammunition ... was obtained from an apparently untouched store, but it was later discovered that this ... had been made in 1941 ... [and] it was impossible to say how long it had been in store in the tropics. (Wilson n.d.: 453–54)

In Wilson's distinctly unscientific series of experiments, a total of 148 rounds were fired from two examples of the 14th Year Type and one example of the Type A Nambu. Test 1 was undertaken with 14th Year Type pistol 86536, maker unknown. Of the 64 rounds fired, 46 fired normally, 17 misfired, and one failed to feed. The test was abandoned after four consecutive misfires. The misfires were transferred to Test 3.

Test 2 was undertaken with the same pistol as Test 1, but the firing-pin spring was replaced. No new springs were available, so one was taken from another of the 14th Year Type specimens. Ten rounds were fired, with all firing normally.

Test 3 was undertaken with 14th Year Type pistol *i*-15846, maker unknown; 33 rounds were fired. In the first trial of the 17 misfires from Test 1, 12 fired normally while five misfired. In the second group of 16 fresh cartridges, 12 fired and four misfired.

Test 4 was undertaken with Type A Nambu 9265, made by TGE. Of the 40 rounds fired, 36 ignited successfully and four misfired.

A typical "Baby" Nambu pistol, accompanied by a 50-round box and two 7×20mm Nambu cartridges: one (left) with a cupro-nickel jacketed bullet and the other (right) a wartime product substituting copper. (Rock Island Auction, www.rockislandauction.com)

Considering his results, Wilson concluded that the tests were largely inconclusive "due chiefly to their rough nature and the fact that the ammunition employed could not be relied upon. However, it seems reasonable to suggest that Test 1 demonstrated a weak and rapidly tiring spring, possibly of poor quality in the first place, also that from the limited data obtained the Nambu behaved better than the Year 14" (Wilson n.d.: 454). Even allowing for the deterioration of the cartridges – and the quality of Japanese propellants was sometimes very poor indeed – the trials clearly showed some of the problems confronting the Japanese soldiery.

Yet so many handguns survived hostilities that a lack of commercially available ammunition became a notable handicap.

Though unsuccessful attempts were made to alter Japanese pistols to use 9mm Parabellum cartridges, increased chamber pressures led to periodic failures, particularly in pistols manufactured late in World War II when the quality of material and manufacture declined. Consequently, the B&E Cartridge Company, Inc., of Minneapolis, founded in 1946 by Robert Edward Bard and Norwegian-born Osborne Wesley ("Ozzie") Klavestad, began to market 8×22mm Nambu cartridges early in 1948. Owing to the absence of conventional die-stamping or metal-drawing machinery, however, B&E cartridge cases had been turned on a multi-spindle lathe. They were loaded with bullets made by die-forming lead-wire segments, which were then given a protective coating of copper alloy.

The Type 100 submachine gun, produced only in small quantities, was the only other weapon to chamber the 8×22mm Nambu cartridge. (Morphy Auctions, www.morphyauctions.com)

The Type 94 pistol was a poorer design in certain respects; at least the locking system of the 14th Year Type was efficient, which could not always be said of its successor. The designers of the Type 94 did manage to eliminate some of the bad features of the earlier 14th Year Type. The latter's suspect firing-pin mechanism was replaced by a powerful internal hammer, and so the Type 94 rarely suffered the misfires that had often characterized its predecessor. The manual and trigger safeties were much better than those of the 14th Year Type but, unfortunately, a new drawback negated each improvement. The strange trigger-and-sear design led to a bad "creepy" trigger pull of between 8.8lb and 9.9lb; and the exposed sear, lying in its channel on the outside of the frame, could be operated simply by striking the front of the bar – without touching the trigger and regardless of whether the magazine safety was engaged.

In addition, the means of achieving disconnection, or ensuring that only a single shot was fired for each pull of the trigger, was efficient only insofar as trigger "clutch" was concerned. The movement of the sear could be impeded externally by pushing or jamming it, thus preventing the disconnection system working. In cases such as these, the slide rolled the hammer back on recoil but the sear tail could not lock satisfactorily in the hammer body; and as the slide returned, the hammer simply rotated forward to rest against the firing pin. The chambered cartridge was rarely ignited as the blow imparted to the inertia-type firing pin was minimal, but there was a slight element of danger.

The chances of the Type 94 pistol firing in cases where the hammer follows the closing stroke of the breech, returning to rest on the head of the firing pin, seems to be slim – unless the cartridges have particularly sensitive primers, when there is potential danger. There is far more danger in striking the exposed sear sufficiently hard to release a fully cocked hammer, as the Type 94 will fire and reload quite normally. A much-voiced theory (now discredited) suggested that the exposed bar permitted Japanese soldiers to commit suicide as they passed their loaded pistols, butt first, to their captors. The pressure required to release the cocked sear is considerable, however, and the bar usually must be struck rather than simply pressed.

The locking system of the Type 94 is theoretically quite efficient, but the poor quality of examples manufactured late in World War II allied with the exposure of the tops of the locking piece in open recesses in the slide-side to cause a number of accidents. Type 94 pistols fired before they were fully locked, or when the lock had worn or jammed. The pistols were consequently transformed into simple blowbacks and damage to components ensued, though this type of malfunction was mercifully rare.

Compared with the older 14th Year Type, the Type 94 has a better safety and a much better ignition system in which a hammer replaced a firing pin; but its trigger-and-sear unit is far worse, and the magazine capacity – a mere six rounds – is too small. Wilson concluded in *Low Velocity Automatic Arms* that:

The designers of the Model 94 clearly set out to ... eliminate the most unsatisfactory features of the Year 14 ... These were, in order of importance, (i) Difficulty of reloading or magazine changing, (ii) Unreliability due to weakness of the striker mechanism, (iii) Difficulty in operating the applied safety device, (iv) Liability of ingress of foreign matter to the action. If success attended the designers' efforts here, in exchange they gave the Model 94 a serious degree of unreliability in function and a risk in operational handling ... the design of the Model 94 is sound with the exception of the firing mechanism. If considered as an intermediate or pocket weapon on account of its size and weight, it ... falls short in comparison with most of its contemporaries in that class. The best that can be said of it is that, from limited interrogation, it was considered ... preferable to the Nambu and Year 14 as an operational weapon. (Wilson n.d.: 469A–69B)

THE NAMBU PISTOLS IN OTHER HANDS

Prior to World War II, only Siam and China are known to have acquired Nambu pistols. The Siamese pistols include several hundred of the original or "Grandpa" variant as well as "Papa'-type handguns, distinguished by the use of a *chakra* (war quoit) as a property mark. Precisely when these pistols were supplied is by no means certain, but they are much more likely to have been acquired at the time of manufacture – in 1905–10 the Japanese were making Siamese "Type 46" Mauser-type rifles, adopted in 1903, in the Koishikawa factory – than as post-1945 reparations. Serial numbers found on Siamese "Grandpa" Nambu pistols lie in the 1559–2296 range, seemingly random, whereas serial numbers of the apparently-few Siamese "Papa" Nambu pistols reported to date are confined to 4556–4692. These pistols have stock slots milled in the backstrap of the butt and one-piece "milled panel" frames, but lack the *Riku shiki* ("Army Type") mark.

Many Nambu pistols will be found with Chinese links, though, once again, details of the acquisitions are scanty. A distinctive "National Army" (國軍) mark has been reported on a variety of "Papa" Nambu pistols: Tōkyō Artillery Arsenal products numbered in the 2519–6875 range, and TGE handguns, some with IJN marks, between 148 and 8414.

It has been suggested that the pistols were used by the army of warlord Zhang Zuolin, who controlled Manchuria from 1916 and was briefly dictator of the Republic of China before being assassinated by men of the pro-Japanese Kwantung Army in 1928. Deployed as mercenaries by the Japanese during the Russo-Japanese War, Zhang and his men ultimately constituted the Fengtian (Zhili) Army: mustering 100,000 men in 1922, this ever-growing force relied on large numbers of weapons that had become available at the close of World War I. It seems probable, therefore, that they included the Nambu pistols, which were ultimately added to the inventory of the newly organized Chinese National Revolutionary Army, the military arm of the Kuomintang from 1925 until 1947.

Many Nambus were lost to Chinese forces during the Second Sino-Japanese War, and then during World War II when guerrilla groups in the Netherlands East Indies – among others – made good use of them.

In addition, when fighting ceased in 1945, large quantities of Japanese handguns were seized not only in the Pacific theater of operations but also in China. Many of these were used to alleviate shortfalls in East Asian armies. Consequently, in addition to the Nambu pistols, 14th Year Type and Type 94 pistols will also be found bearing the Siamese/Thai *chakra* or the Chinese National Army property mark (國軍).

Substantial numbers of 14th Year Type pistols seized from Japanese units serving in what was to become Indonesia were converted to fire the 9×19mm Parabellum cartridge. The alterations were effected by fitting the barrel of a KNIL M1911 Luger after suitable modifications had been made by cutting the Japanese 8mm barrel to a stub, cutting a suitable thread in the remaining portion, and then threading or "sweating" the Luger barrel in place. Others seem to have been fitted with entirely new barrels, often somewhat longer than the original

Two members of the Dutch East Indies irregulars, active during the Japanese occupation, inspect a 14th Year Type pistol. (Australian War Memorial 017626, www.awm.gov.au)

Japanese pattern, work that is presumed to have been undertaken by what had become the Tentara Nasional Indonesia (TNI, Indonesian National Army) after the 1949 revolution once supplies of M1911-type 9mm barrels ran short.

When the Korean War began in June 1950, the 14th Year Type pistol was among the most commonly encountered handguns arming the Chinese Communist forces even though Russian/Soviet Nagant and Japanese 26th Year Type revolvers, Soviet Tokarev pistols, the Mauser C/96 (together with a variety of clones and copies), and the American M1911A1 Colt-Browning were also used in quantity. The North Korean military authorities refurbished many 14th Year Type pistols in this period, often mixing components indiscriminately. According to marks on the inner surface of the grips, the work was undertaken in Zinizu Arsenal on the Yalu River. A five-point star also generally appears.

Many Nambu-type pistols survived to be used in the First Indochina War (1946–54) and then the Vietnam War (1955–75), though numbers declined as those conflicts ran their course. No refurbishment programs are known to have been undertaken in this era; shortened pistols have been reported occasionally, but most have simply had their damaged barrels repaired.

This fascinating 14th Year Type pistol, Nagoya-Toriimatsu *ro-*59349 dating from October 1944 (Shōwa 19.10), was recovered from Vietnam in the 1960s. It has been altered to chamber the 7.62×25mm Tokarev cartridge, using a barrel taken from what was probably a .30-caliber Luger. (Saigon 1965@flickr.com)

DESIGN INFLUENCE

The Nambu pistol has had very little direct effect on handgun design outside Japan – but there is a notable exception. On November 5, 1946, William Batterman Ruger of Wilton, Connecticut, applied for a US patent to protect a pistol. Born in 1916, Ruger had developed a light machine gun tested by the US Army in 1938 as the T10. Though little came of the project, Ruger had been hired by the Ordnance Department to work at Springfield Armory, where the machine gun became the T23E1.

Shortly after the end of World War II, Ruger acquired a Nambu pistol that had been brought back from the Pacific theater of operations by a US Marine. Impressed, he promptly embarked on incorporating elements of the design in a small-caliber blowback pistol made in his garage. Claims to novelty included simplifying production by making the frame from two heavy-duty steel pressings or stampings welded together, and by using a tubular receiver to receive a cylindrical breech-bolt.

The grant of US patent 2655839, "Blowback Autoloading Pistol," was delayed until October 20, 1953, probably because claims to novelty may have been contested by Ruger's competitors. The patent-drawings show a pistol with a parallel-sided grip, but Ruger and his entrepreneurial partner Alexander McCormick Sturm had meanwhile created Sturm, Ruger & Company to make the .22 pistol in quantity.

US Registered Design 164735, sought in April 1950, had been granted on October 2, 1951, to protect the refinement of the grip. Interestingly,

Ruger acknowledged the influence not of the Nambu but only of the German Tell air pistol, the Colt Woodsman, and the Luger. The omission may simply suggest, however, that praising anything Japanese would have been regarded at the time as a handicap to sales.

Regrettably, Alexander Sturm died in November 1951, aged only 28, without ever seeing the runaway success of the Ruger Standard pistol – which can still be obtained in a modernized Mk IV form not too dissimilar from Ruger's 1949 prototype.

This .22 rimfire Ruger Standard pistol dates from 1958. (Morphy Auctions, www.morphyauctions.com)

This long-barreled version of the .22 Ruger Standard pistol, made in 1965, is intended for target-shooting. (Morphy Auctions, www.morphyauctions.com)

SUCCESSORS

When World War II ended, the Allied occupation forces disarmed the Japanese. Military personnel, police, and even civilians were forced to give up their firearms in all but exceptional circumstances; for a while, police carried nothing but old military swords while on duty. When war began in Korea in June 1950, however, attitudes changed dramatically; just as in Europe, where the German Bundeswehr (armed forces) was formed to counter what was perceived to be Soviet aggression, so the Allies realized that Japan was also vulnerable to Chinese and Soviet threats.

In July 1950, therefore, with the support of the Allied occupation authorities, the Japanese government created a 75,000-strong National Police Reserve (*Keisatsu yobitai*). A Coastal Safety Force (*Kaijō keibitai*) followed in 1952 after a security treaty signed on September 8, 1951 allowed US forces to deal with external aggression, while new Japanese ground and maritime forces coped with internal threats and natural disasters. In mid-1952 the National Safety Force (*Kokka anzen butai*) – soon redesignated the National Security Force (*Kokka anzen hoshōbutai*) – was created by enlarging the National Police Reserve to 110,000 men, while the Coastal Safety Force effectively became an embryonic navy. Finally, on July 1, 1954, the National Security Force became the Ground Self-Defense Force, the Coastal Safety Force became the Maritime Self-Defense Force, and the Air Self-Defense Force was authorized.

New Nambu 57A. Intended for the Japanese armed forces and the coast guard, the New Nambu Model 57A was essentially a scaled-down M1911 Colt-Browning chambered for the 9mm Parabellum cartridge, while the Model 57B was a 7.65mm blowback pistol loosely based on the 1910-type FN-Browning but with an exposed hammer replacing the concealed firing pin. (Author's archives)

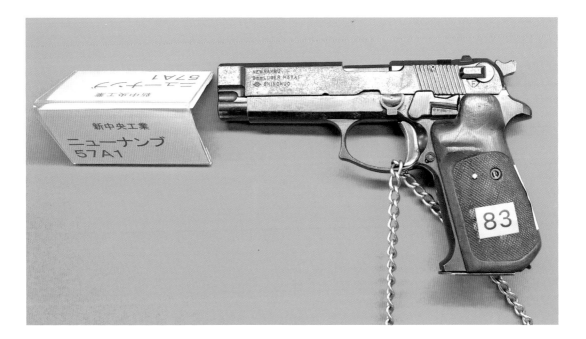

An M57A1 prototype at the JGSDF Ordnance School in Tsuchiura. (Dragoner JP/ Wikimedia/CC BY-SA 4.0)

Owing to the confiscation and dispersal of wartime equipment, firearms were required in quantity. As far as handguns were concerned, Allied weaponry was issued to the Japanese police from 1949 onward. Handguns included the ubiquitous .45 M1911A1 Colt-Browning, which was not popular owing to its weight and recoil, together with a variety of .38 revolvers including the Colt Official Police Model and the Smith & Wesson Military & Police Model.

Maritime Safety Agency (coast guard) personnel were issued with 14th Year Type pistols – perhaps as many as 1,000 – until the manufacture of 8×22mm Nambu cartridges ceased in the 1960s. The pistols were then replaced, apparently with Japanese-made revolvers.

So great was the need for handguns, however, that development began again in Japan. The principal contractor was Shin-Chūō Kogyo, often characterized as a lineal successor of the Nambu-Seisakusho business, which produced the .38 Smith & Wesson-like New Nambu Model 60 revolver, adopted by the National Police Agency in 1960, alongside 7.65mm and 9mm New Nambu Model 57 pistols. Limited production of the 57A and 57B patterns was undertaken in the late 1950s, but neither was especially successful. The authorities in both Japan and the United States determined to maintain standardization of weapons and equipment where practicable, and so the .45 Colt-Browning was widely retained.

When the Joint Service Small Arms Program (JSSAP) trials with 9mm handguns began in the United States in the 1970s, however, the Japanese recommenced trials with what had become the New Nambu 57A1. Success still eluded the New Nambu pistol, though, as the 9mm SIG-Sauer P220 was duly adopted in 1982 (the earliest pistols were bought in Europe, but are now manufactured by Minebea as the P9); and Model 60 revolver production ceased in 1999 after about 133,400 had been manufactured.

CONCLUSION

There are many differing opinions of the Nambu, the 14th Year Type, and the Type 94, most of which are uncomplimentary. The most damning is Wilson's, but he had at least taken the opportunity to assess the value of the Japanese pistols under combat conditions. It is unfair, however, to decry the Japanese pistols solely on the grounds that they were poorly made. German and Soviet manufacturers were also responsible for some notably badly made weapons, particularly when manufacture and production had become chaotic through heavy bombing or wholesale relocation. Occasionally, small arms made apparently crudely functioned better in adverse conditions than others made to the finest tolerance – the different performances of the German MG 34 and MG 42 general-purpose machine guns being cases in point – and many Soviet weapons were manufactured in an environment in which reliability of function was prioritized over quality of finish.

In addition, Japanese troops, including many junior officers, paid virtually no attention to field maintenance of their weapons – a point clearly stressed in many Allied wartime intelligence manuals. The weapons and their ammunition, therefore, tended to deteriorate much more rapidly than comparable Western equipment and the inference was easily (but often wrongly) drawn that the standard of Japanese weapons manufacture was markedly inferior.

The Type 94 pistol was a poorer design in certain respects; at least the locking system of the 14th Year Type pistol was efficient, which could not always be said of its successor. In addition, the 14th Year Type does have noteworthy features, though in practice they scarcely offset its many serious deficiencies. The features include a light and pleasant trigger pull, acceptable combat sights, reasonable accuracy, and – above all – light recoil. US Army trials conducted in 1948 indicated that the 14th Year Type was more accurate than the US Colt M1911A1, the German Walther P 38, and the Soviet Tokarev. Yet faint praise cannot excuse the truly execrable features of the 14th Year Type and Type 94, the worst of which was undoubtedly the former's weak firing-pin spring.

BIBLIOGRAPHY

Bramois, Francis (1976). "Les Pistolets Nambu de l'Armée Impériale Japonaise," *Gazette des Armes* 34: 8–12.

Brown, James D. (2007). *Collector's Guide to Imperial Japanese Handguns 1893–1945*. Atglen, PA: Schiffer Publishing.

Derby, Harry (1981). *The Hand Cannons of Imperial Japan*. Charlotte, NC: Derby Publishing.

Derby, Harry L. III, & Brown, James D. (2003). *Japanese Military Cartridge Handguns 1893–1945*. Atglen, PA: Schiffer Publishing.

Honeycutt, Fred L., Jr (1982). *Military Pistols of Japan*. Lake Park, FL: Julin Books.

Kotrba, William, Jr (1971). "Japanese Used Early Nambu Pistols in Many Conflicts," *The American Rifleman*, March 1971: 23–25.

Kotrba, William, Jr (1973). "Nambu Flaws Trimmed in Type 14," *The American Rifleman*, July 1973: 54–57.

Leithe, Frederick E. (1967). *Japanese Handguns*. Alhambra, CA: Borden Publishing.

Markham, George (1977). "The Japanese Nambu and 14th Year Type Pistols, Part I. The Nambu Pistols/The "Baby" Nambu," *Shooter's Bible* 68: 55–61.

Markham, George (1978). "The Japanese Nambu and 14th Year Type Pistols, Part II. Taisho 14th Year Type Pistol/Large-magazine Nambu Prototype," *Shooter's Bible* 69: 37–46.

Markham, George & Walter, John D. (1980). "The Japanese Nambu Pistols," *Guns Review*, November 1980: 845–49.

Moss, John L. (1975). "Japanese Autoloading Pistols," *Guns Digest*, 29th Edition, 69–77.

Wilson, Robert K. (no date). *Low Velocity Automatic Arms, Chapter X, The Japanese Group of Pistols*. Unpublished multi-volume manuscript.

Wilson, Robert K., with Hogg, Ian V. (1975). *Textbook of Automatic Pistols*. London: Arms & Armour Press.

This 14th Year Type pistol, fitted with the post-1940 enlarged trigger guard, displays the Nagoya-Toriimatsu maker's mark ahead of the serial number *ro*-15472 on the right-side rear of the frame, above Shōwa 19.2, revealing the date of manufacture to be February 1944. The left side of the slide displays the designation *Ju-yon nenshiki* ("14th Year Type") below the back sight and firing instructions above the safety lever. (Morphy Auctions, www.morphyauctions.com)

INDEX

Figures in **bold** refer to illustrations.